HAWAIIAN INSECTS
AND THEIR KIN

Published in North America by
University of Hawaii Press
2840 Kolowalu Street
Honolulu, Hawaii 96822

Simultaneously published in Singapore by
Times Editions Pte Ltd
Times Centre
1 New Industrial Road
Singapore 1953
© 1992 Times Editions Pte Ltd

Printed in Singapore

Library of Congress Cataloging-in-Publication Data
Howarth, Francis G., 1940–
        Hawaiian insects and their kin/Francis G. Howarth and William P.
Mull.
                p.   cm.
        Includes bibliographical references and index.
        ISBN 0-8248-1469-X
        1. Insects—Hawaii. I. Mull, William P., 1921–   . II. Title.
QL489.H3H68   1992
595.709969—dc20   91-48257
                                                           CIP

Frontispiece: *Nabis curtipennis* female.

HAWAIIAN INSECTS AND THEIR KIN

Francis G. Howarth
and
William P. Mull

University of Hawaii Press
Honolulu

Contents

INTRODUCTION

Insects hardly need an introduction; they are everywhere and familiar to everyone. Most people can easily recognize the major groups of insects, such as beetles, flies, wasps, and moths. Yet the bewildering array of different kinds of insects often overwhelms both scientist and layperson. In addition, there are many related animals—such as spiders, mites, millipedes, and centipedes—that are not true insects. So let us begin with an introduction to the main characters in this book.

Insects and their relatives make up the group of invertebrates (animals without backbones) that have a stiff external skeleton and segmented legs and body parts. This group is appropriately called the arthropods (jointed feet). This book covers the insects and terrestrial (living on land) arthropods of Hawai'i. It does not cover the marine arthropods (for example, crabs, shrimps, barnacles). We emphasize native species (those whose ancestors came without the aid of humans and are found naturally in Hawai'i), but we include some foreign species (introduced either purposely or inadvertently by humans). Native species include both endemic species (those occurring naturally only in Hawai'i) and indigenous species (those occurring in Hawai'i as well as elsewhere).

Insects are by far the dominant arthropods in Hawai'i. In fact, 95% of the 5,565 described species of native terrestrial arthropods are insects. The native insect fauna is estimated to exceed 10,000 species, so we are not even close to a complete survey of that fauna. About 2,700 insect species and 560 other land arthropod species in Hawai'i are alien.

All questions on arthropods cannot be fully answered in this book. Questions like "What kind of insect is that?" or "What does it do?" and "Is it harmful?" or "Is it helpful?" can only be partly answered. Our purpose is to make known some of the dominant groups making up one of the most unique insect faunas anywhere on earth, to show how the study of these insects is improving our general understanding of evolution and ecology, to dispel the fear of meeting an unknown animal, and to show the excitement of studying insects and their relatives.

We dedicate this book to the memory of Dr Wayne C. Gagné (top, in a lava tube) and Mae E. Mull (bottom, at Alaka'i Swamp), whose friendship, expertise in science and environmental education, and dedication to conservation of native Hawaiian biota provided much inspiration for this book.

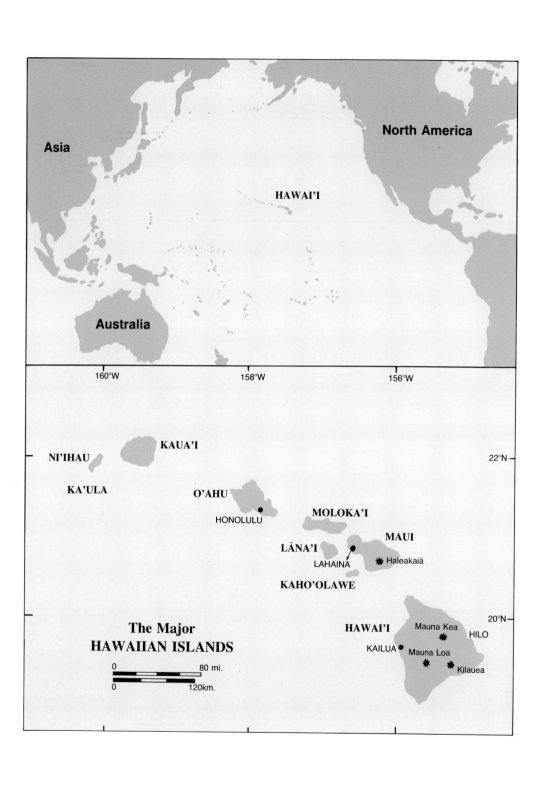

Asia

North America

HAWAI'I

Australia

NI'IHAU   KAUA'I

KA'ULA   O'AHU

22°N

HONOLULU

MOLOKA'I

LĀNA'I   MAUI

LAHAINA   Haleakaiā

KAHO'OLAWE

20°N

The Major
HAWAIIAN ISLANDS

HAWAI'I   Mauna Kea   HILO

KAILUA   Mauna Loa

0   80 mi.

0   120km.

Kilauea

FEATURES OF
THE HAWAIIAN ISLANDS

THE GEOLOGY OF HAWAI'I

The Hawaiian Islands, with a total land area of 16,710 square kilometers (6,420 square miles), extend 2,400 kilometers (1,500 miles) across the north-central Pacific Ocean from the island of Hawai'i to Kure Atoll and are the most isolated group of high islands on earth. They are about 3,800 kilometers (2,300 miles) west of continental North America and the same distance from the nearest neighboring high islands, the Marquesas in French Polynesia.

The Hawaiian Islands are the summits of giant submarine volcanoes coming from a hot spot beneath the Pacific Tectonic Plate. The hot spot has been relatively stationary through time, producing volcanoes in assembly-line fashion as the Pacific Plate moved northwest. Each island or group of islands is progressively older in a northwest direction, and each has always been isolated from the others by deep straits at least 40 kilometers (25 miles) wide.

The island chain began over 70 million years ago and is made up of three groups: the youngest eight main islands with their offshore islets at the southeast end, the relict

The major Hawaiian islands.

volcanic islands and coral atolls (about 6 to 30 million years old) in the middle, and a long chain of progressively older and sunken seamounts extending north of Kure Atoll to the Aleutian Trench. At least some of the last group, the Emperor Seamounts, were once above sea level and could have been stepping stones for some of the current Hawaiian biota.

Starting at the southeast end of the chain is the island of Hawai'i. It is also called the Big Island and is the youngest (probably less than 700,000 years old), largest (10,458 square kilometers or 4,038 square miles in area), and highest (4,205 meters or 13,796 feet above sea level) of the main islands. It was formed by five volcanoes: Kohala, Mauna Kea, Hualālai, Mauna Loa, and Kīlauea. Mauna Kea (4,205 meters or 13,796 feet) bears the scars of past glaciers and broke the ocean surface some 380,000 years ago. Mauna Loa (4,169 meters or 13,677 feet) and Kīlauea (1,248 meters or 4,093 feet) are still very active.

Northwest of the Big Island is the island complex consisting of six volcanoes on four islands (Maui, Kaho'olawe, Lāna'i, and Moloka'i). These islands, sometimes called Maui Nui, have been separated from

9

each other through rising sea level, sinking land, and erosion.

Next is O'ahu, formed by two volcanoes 2.6 to 3.7 million years ago. The highest ridges of O'ahu are sharply eroded and rise up to 1,225 meters or 4,020 feet.

Kaua'i is the oldest of the main islands but, compared to the continents, it is still relatively young, being less than 5.5 million years old. It rises nearly 1,600 meters or 5,243 feet above the sea. The summit of Kaua'i is considered to be the wettest spot on earth, with an annual rainfall sometimes over 1,500 cm (600 inches).

THE NORTHWESTERN HAWAIIAN ISLANDS

Most of the northwestern Hawaiian Islands, from Nihoa to Kure, are administered by the United States Fish and Wildlife Service as a wildlife sanctuary. The insect faunas of these low islands are still relatively unknown, yet many representatives of groups that were once part of the lowland insect fauna of the main islands still survive there.

Insects associated with sea birds and coastal habitats on these islands are often widely distributed on other Pacific islands. Also, endemic members of many typical Hawaiian insect groups are, or were at one time, found on these islands, indicating a stepping-stone progression of the fauna along the chain.

ECOSYSTEMS AND VEGETATION ZONES

The Hawaiian Islands support a remarkable number of different habitats due to their diverse topography and climate. The high islands intercept moisture from storms and prevailing trade winds, creating extreme differences in annual rainfall, which can vary between 25 cm (10 inches) on leeward coasts to over 1,000 cm (400 inches) at mid-elevation windward areas only a few miles away. Also, habitats are zoned by altitude above sea level, with cooler climates at higher elevations.

The major vegetation zones in the Hawaiian Islands are littoral (on both rocky and sandy shores), strand plant communities, lowland dry scrub, desert, grassland, partly deciduous dry forest, mesic forest, and (on the windward sides of the higher islands) lowland rain forest grading into a montane rain forest near 900 meters (3,000 feet).

On the higher mountains, a cool dry forest or savannah (mountain parkland) occurs above 1,500 meters (5,000 feet), which grades into alpine scrub above 2,000 meters (7,000 feet) and a stone desert bearing an aeolian (feeding on organic matter blown in from elsewhere) community above 3,000 meters (10,000 feet).

The boundaries of these vegetation zones are dictated by climate, local topography, type of lava, age, soil development, altitude, and degree of human disturbance. Since communities of plants and animals exploiting these habitats developed independently on each island, each island harbors its own unique communities.

More than 100 different native plant communities have been recognized, and examples of almost all of the world's major kinds of plant communities exist within the islands. Aquatic communities live in pools, lakes, and streams. Young, unvegetated lava flows in each climatic regime sustain aeolian communities, and lava tubes and other voids in

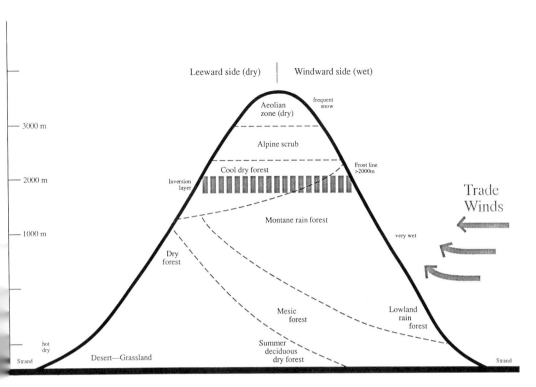

Leeward side (dry) | Windward side (wet)

Aeolian zone (dry)

frequent snow

3000 m

Alpine scrub

Cool dry forest

Frost line >2000m

Inversion layer

2000 m

Trade Winds

Montane rain forest

1000 m

very wet

Dry forest

Mesic forest

Lowland rain forest

Summer deciduous dry forest

hot dry

Strand

Desert—Grassland

Strand

young lava support diverse communities of cave animals.

More than 150 distinct natural ecosystems (i.e., each of them a discrete group of interacting species in a common area) are found in the Hawaiian Islands. This is comparable to the number of ecosystems typically found in continental areas. It underscores the ecological richness of Hawai'i.

A generalized cross-section through a higher Hawaiian mountain showing the relationship between the trade winds and major vegetation zones.

View of windward Mauna Kea from the sea to the snow-capped summit. The light green lowland is mostly sugar cane with incursions of mixed native and introduced forests along stream gullies. The middle dark band is native **'ōhi'a lehua** *rain forest. The upper bands are mixed pasture and native* **koa** *forest,* **māmane** *savannah, alpine shrub, and aeolian stone desert.*

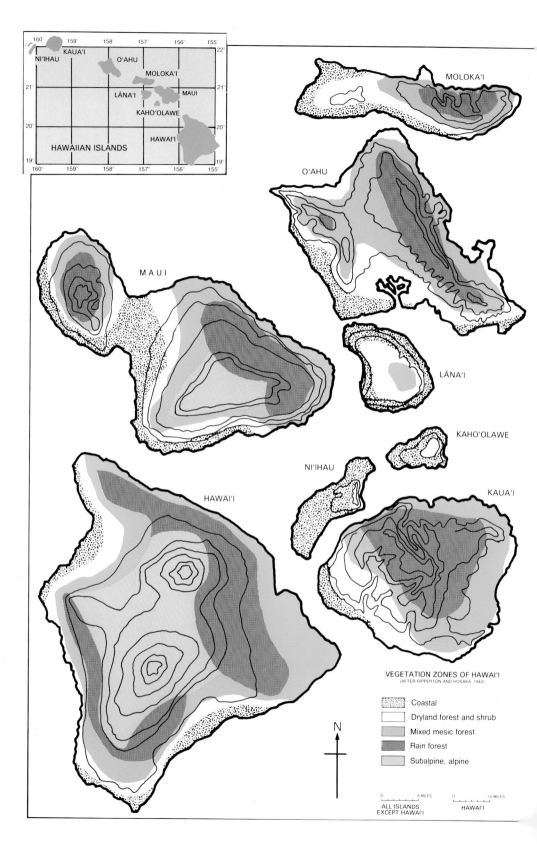

HAWAIIAN ISLANDS

VEGETATION ZONES OF HAWAI'I
(AFTER RIPPERTON AND HOSAKA 1942)

Coastal

Dryland forest and shrub

Mixed mesic forest

Rain forest

Subalpine, alpine

N

0   6 MILES
ALL ISLANDS
EXCEPT HAWAI'I

0   10 MILES
HAWAI'I

A BRIEF HISTORY OF HAWAIIAN ENTOMOLOGY

Early Polynesians knew of native insects and undoubtedly developed many cultural and oral traditions about these creatures of the Hawaiian Islands. The Hawaiian creation chant mentions many native insects—dragonfly nymphs were used in rituals, and native moth caterpillars still are *'aumākua* (guardian spirits) for some Hawaiian families.

Hawai'i was the first country to put a picture of a butterfly on a postage stamp, in a two-cent issue in 1891. Unfortunately, many Hawaiian traditions about insects were lost before they could be recorded. One that did survive involves the existence of a large cricket-like animal, called the *'ūhini pa'awela*, in the Ka'ū District of the Big Island; it was a favorite food among the Hawaiians there until the late 1800s. A few of these animals roasted on a skewer provided a full meal. No specimens of the *'ūhini pa'awela* survived, and we can only speculate that it may have been a giant weta-like *Banza* katydid or a *Thaumatogryllus* cricket.

Historic knowledge of Hawaiian biology developed during three periods: the exploration period (1778–1850), the resident naturalist period (1820–1900), and the modern

Vegetation zones of Hawai'i.

period (1890–present). Unfortunately, arthropods were neglected by most of the early explorers, and even specimens taken back to Europe and North America were ignored by scientists. Insects were collected by naturalists on Captain Cook's initial voyage to Hawai'i in 1778–1779, but the only insects described were two wasps: Plants, snails, and birds captured the curiosity of the early naturalists, and a myth developed (which at first proved hard to dispel) that few insects existed on oceanic islands.

Entomological studies began in earnest with the arrival of the first resident naturalist to concentrate on insects, the Reverend Thomas Blackburn, who lived in Hawai'i from 1877 to 1883. He supplied scientists at the British Museum in London and elsewhere with a steady stream of specimens, refuting the belief that insects were poorly represented in Hawai'i. Unfortunately, many of Blackburn's species have not been re-collected. Human activity and invasion by alien biota, especially cattle and other ungulates, destroyed many of the lowland native communities before insects were seriously collected. We owe much of our understanding of the native lowland insect fauna to Blackburn's work.

The modern period of Hawaiian entomology began just before the turn of the century with the arrival of professionally trained scientists. Growing awareness of the diverse and unique fauna, as well as the specter of extinction of native species, led to the commissioning of a faunal survey sponsored jointly by the Royal Society of London and the British Association for the Advancement of Science, in collaboration with the Bishop Museum of Honolulu. British entomologist R.C.L. Perkins was hired for the formidable task of conducting the survey's fieldwork that eventually resulted in the multivolume *Fauna Hawaiiensis*, edited by David Sharp.

From 1892 to the early 1900s, Perkins made truly remarkable collections of many groups, concentrating especially on beetles, moths, wasps, and damselflies. Only a few groups, including flies, true bugs, and spiders, were not covered as thoroughly. His ability to procure good material and identify species in the field is legendary, and his accounts include a wealth of biological information. *Fauna Hawaiiensis* remains the baseline of our knowledge of many Hawaiian arthropod groups.

The Bernice Pauahi Bishop Museum, founded in 1889, was instrumental in providing local support for Perkins and *Fauna Hawaiiensis*, and in encouraging other biological surveys of the islands. Still the premier natural history institution in the islands, its Hawaiian insect collection consists of nearly one million specimens, and contains representatives of more than three-quarters of the described species. In addition to the early historical material, especially from *Fauna Hawaiiensis*, the collection has a wealth of newer material. Significant historical collections from Hawai'i are also found at the British Museum (Natural History)—the primary depository for voucher material from the *Fauna Hawaiiensis* survey—the Hawaii State Department of Agriculture, and the University of Hawaii at Manoa.

In the late 1800s, plantation agriculture was an important economic base, and newly arriving alien insect pests were a continual concern, especially to the expanding sugarcane plantations. In 1893, the government of Hawai'i hired Albert Koebele, who had just established a successful pest control program in California using alien insect predators. Koebele traveled throughout the world, sending back alien species to Hawai'i. He is credited with introducing hundreds of beneficial species for biological control. It was a grandiose experiment in ecology, but accurate records of specific introductions, their fate, and the resulting impacts on the native biota were not kept.

Early successes with biological control encouraged the Hawaiian Sugar Planters' Association (HSPA) to begin its own program in 1904. For more than half a century, the HSPA was the largest employer of entomologists in Hawai'i. A number of prominent entomologists passed through its ranks, including R.C.L. Perkins, O.H. Swezey, F.X. Williams, and E.C. Zimmerman.

The biological control program in Hawai'i continues today under the aegis of the Hawaii State Department of Agriculture. Between 1890 and 1985, the documented intentional introductions and releases into the state totaled 639 species of arthropods, of which 230 became established.

The Hawaiian Entomological Society, founded in 1906, is one of the oldest entomological societies in the United States. The annual *Proceedings of the Hawaiian Entomological Society* and publications by the

Bishop Museum Press and the University of Hawaii Press have been the principal outlets for Hawaiian entomological research since *Fauna Hawaiiensis*.

In addition to their duties at the HSPA, Perkins, Swezey, Williams, Zimmerman, and others conducted studies on the biology of native Hawaiian insects. The results from Swezey's work, which spanned 50 years, were collated in *Forest Entomology in Hawaii*, which continues to be the primary source of host data for many Hawaiian groups, especially moths. Williams published well-illustrated and very readable accounts on aquatic insects, native and alien sugarcane insects, and other groups.

In 1934, Zimmerman, while working at the Bishop Museum and the HSPA, began cataloging the Hawaiian insect fauna, which led to the monumental series, *Insects of Hawaii*. Fourteen volumes were published between 1948 and 1981. Only the large orders of Hymenoptera (wasps) and Coleoptera (beetles) have not been treated. Volume I by Zimmerman remains the best overall treatment of the natural history of Hawaii. D. Elmo Hardy, at the University of Hawaii, joined the project in 1949 and, in collaboration with students and specialists, published accounts of the Diptera (true flies) in volumes 10 to 14. The 450% increase in the described Diptera fauna between 1948 and 1989 resulted from Hardy's strong encouragement of systematic studies.

A male **Eupithecia orichloris** *from Lāna'i, showing the characteristic green color. Its caterpillar is a predator.*

ORIGIN OF THE HAWAIIAN INSECT FAUNA

The extreme isolation and young age of the islands severely limited the number of plants and animals that found their own way to Hawai'i. Only those organisms that could disperse across vast oceanic distances and establish reproducing populations became successful colonizers. In fact, only 350–400 separate colonizations can account for the total Hawaiian insect fauna. This means that during the 70 million years of the existence of the island chain, only one successful long-distance dispersal event every 175,000 years was necessary. Even if all 400 arrived during the age of the present islands (30 million years), only one successful arrival every 75,000 years could account for just the insect fauna alone. These are conservative estimates since there have been many extinctions, but long-distance dispersal and successful colonization are certainly rare events.

Many groups typically found in continental areas are missing, and many biologists visiting the islands are at first struck by what is not present. Only about 50% of the known orders (see Table 1) and just 15% of

The older high volcanoes support a diverse array of aquatic habitats. Here, a large tributary joins the upper Wainiha River on Kaua'i.

the known families of insects are represented in the native fauna. Large, showy species and the primitive, flightless, moisture-loving soil forms are poorly represented. For example, there are no native chrysomelid, scarabaeid, or buprestid beetles, swallowtail butterflies, termites, short-horned grasshoppers, cockroaches, mayflies, stoneflies, horse flies, deer flies, bumble bees, sawflies, or ants. However, representatives of many of these groups are now present, having arrived through human-aided transport (see Table 1).

The native terrestrial fauna is composed primarily of three characteristically mobile groups: arthropods (especially insects), land snails, and birds. Many living things no doubt arrived only to find a hostile environment; or they were unable to reproduce, so they perished. But some did win the dispersal sweepstakes and established populations in the islands. Those arriving by air flew, rode on birds, or drifted with the wind. Those arriving by sea swam, drifted with the currents, or came on floating debris. Wind, especially storms and jet streams, appears to have carried most of the successful arthropods to the islands. The ancestors of most native insects belong to the same groups that are now

17

Table 1. *Summary of Hawaiian land and freshwater arthropods.*

Order (common name)	Endemic species[1]	Indigenous species[2]	Alien species[3]
ARACHNIDA (spiders & relatives)			
Palpigradi (palpigrades)			1
Pseudoscorpiones (false scorpions)	4		6
Scorpiones (scorpions)			1
Schizomida (schizomids)			1
Acari[4] (mites & ticks)	93	7	414
Araneae[4] (spiders)	(154)[5]		73
CRUSTACEA (crabs & relatives)			
Amphipoda[4] (sandhoppers)	6	1	2
Isopoda[4] (sowbugs)	9	9	25
MYRIAPODA (myriapods)			
Diplopoda[4] (millipedes)	17		9
Chilopoda[4] (centipedes)	4?		22
Pauropoda (pauropods)			2
Symphyla (symphylans)			4
INSECTA (insects)			
Protura (proturans)			1
Collembola[4] (springtails)	(50)		78
Entotrophi (diplurans)	?		4
Microcoryphia (bristletails)	3		
Thysanura (silverfish)	?		6
Ephemeroptera (mayflies)			3
Odonata (dragonflies & damselflies)	32	2	6
Orthoptera[4] (crickets & katydids)	(220)	1	27
Blattaria (cockroaches)			20
Mantodea (mantids)			6
Dermaptera (earwigs)	7	1	12
Isoptera (termites)			6
Embiidina (webspinners)			2
Zoraptera (zorapterans)			1
Psocoptera[4] (barklice)	75	5	41
Mallophaga[4] (chewing lice)	5	15	47
Anoplura (sucking lice)			14
Thysanoptera (thrips)	29	?	121
Heteroptera[4] (true bugs)	(272)	2	103
Homoptera[4] (hoppers, scales, etc.)	378	?	294
Neuroptera[4] (lacewings)	51		8
Coleoptera[4] (beetles)	1355	7	640
Strepsiptera (stylopids)			4
Trichoptera (caddisflies)			3
Lepidoptera[4] (moths & butterflies)	867		194
Diptera[4] (true flies)	1121	10	431
Siphonaptera (fleas)	1		9
Hymenoptera[4] (wasps, bees, & ants)	647	5	624
TOTAL	5500	65	3265

Source: Nishida & Miller, 1990.

[1] Endemic refers to species naturally occurring only in Hawai'i.

[2] Indigenous refers to species naturally occurring in Hawai'i and elsewhere.

[3] Alien refers to species both inadvertently and purposely introduced.

[4] Include groups in which a significant number of additional species are known but not yet described.

[5] Parentheses include new species being described.

often found dispersing in wind currents on the continents. These include small flies, beetles, wasps, moths, bugs, leafhoppers, and planthoppers. There are few living fossils or relict groups, a fact that also emphasizes the youth of the islands. The oceanic distances to Hawai'i have always been so vast that, with the exception of saltwater-loving species, the sea was a poor avenue for dispersal. But a surprising number of marine groups were able to invade freshwater and even terrestrial habitats in Hawai'i. In fact, most of the native freshwater species probably arrived by sea.

By tradition, marine biologists do not study insects, and entomologists usually start their studies above the high-tide mark; thus few biologists realize that shallow marine habitats are often teeming with insects. About half of the insect orders are represented there, and many of these marine groups were able to drift or raft to Hawai'i.

Once a successful population established itself on any one of the Hawaiian Islands it could disperse much more easily from island to island in stepping-stone fashion. So newly emerging islands in the growing chain received colonists from neighboring older islands, and—very infrequently—from locations much farther away.

Hawai'i, being in the northern mid-Pacific, has received these long-distance dispersers from all points of the compass, but the strong ocean and air currents that parallel the equator greatly restricted successful dispersal from the southern hemisphere. The majority arrived from the Orient and could have island-hopped across part of the Western Pacific. A large percentage belong to north temperate groups and could have come from either Asia or North America.

Closeup of O'ahu flightless crane fly **Limonia hardyana***, showing its minute wings.*

HAWAIIAN INSECT EVOLUTION

Insects that successfully established populations evolved to exploit the full range of habitats available. In fact, the 350–400 separate colonizers evolved into a total estimated insect fauna of about 10,000 endemic species, meaning that, on average, each colonizing species gave rise to 25 new species.

The average number of new species arising per colonization is smaller in native plants, birds, and snails, but the pattern of only a few colonizers giving rise to many closely related species is an important characteristic of the Hawaiian biota. Some colonists apparently did not speciate at all, while others diverged into more than 100 different species. How this occurred has been the subject of much speculation and research, and the results of these Hawaiian studies are adding important insights into worldwide patterns in ecology and evolution.

The evolution of the Hawaiian insects has paralleled the geological history of the islands. The six largest islands, with their great diversity of habitats and species, present ideal evolutionary laboratories. Each island acts as a mini-continent, having obtained its biota from across-water dispersal, and each is a microcosm of evolutionary and ecological processes on the continents.

The isolation of the islands from each other—sequential ages, and sequential development of similar climatic zones, habitats, and ecosystems on each island, along with the formation of isolating barriers within each by erosion and volcanism—has favored rapid speciation. Biologists now believe the formation of a new species usually follows the founding of a new population isolated from its parent population. This would happen when one or a few individuals colonized a new island. Being small, the founding population would carry only part of the genetic variation of its parent population; also, new selection forces, different from those experienced by its parent population, would act on the new population.

As mutations occurred and the founding population expanded and adapted to its surroundings, the new population would diverge from its parental population and, over time, become a new species. This process was repeated on each new island in the chain.

Sometimes a small change in

A male Big Island picture-wing, **Drosophila conspicua***, stands next to the cosmopolitan vinegar fly,* **D. melanogaster***.*

behavior or form allowed a species to exploit a totally different resource or habitat from that of its ancestors. These changes are called "adaptive shifts." A new population created by an adaptive shift may disperse up and down the island chain, giving rise to additional new species. Both speciation and adaptive shifts have been recurring within the islands, creating swarms of closely related species. Hawai'i is one of the best places for studying the results of this process, known as "adaptive radiation."

Evolution within some groups has been explosive: there are over 600 species of Hawaiian flies in the genus *Drosophila* and between 350 and 500 species of moths in the genus *Hyposmocoma*. Seven other genera also contain more than 100 native species (see Table 2). Many more genera will join the 100-member list when additional systematic studies are completed.

The vast majority of the native arthropod species of Hawai'i are endemic to single islands, or even to individual volcanoes or small areas within single islands. These evolutionary processes have great predictive value. One can find new species on an unusual host or in an unusual habitat and successfully predict that a close relative exploits a similar niche on the neighboring islands. This has been done on several occasions recently in studies of specific insect groups.

The theory that small populations would contain less variation than larger populations led to the idea that island species must be less variable than continental ones. But the Hawaiian species studied to date have at least as much variation in some genetic characteristics as species elsewhere. Variation, of course, provides the raw material for natural selection in the evolutionary process.

By coincidence, the cosmopolitan vinegar fly, *Drosophila melanogaster*, has been the most popular organism for teaching and studying genetics for nearly a century. In the 1950s, when D. Elmo Hardy began describing the fantastic diversity of native *Drosophila*, he realized that a marvelous natural evolutionary experiment was occurring in the island forests. It was as if an earlier geneticist had locked specimens of a close relative of *Drosophila melanogaster* in a number of extremely large test tubes and allowed them to evolve for thousands or even millions of years.

Thus, in 1963, the Hawaiian Drosophila Project began deciphering the genetics and evolution of this amazing group of flies. Over 800 species of Drosophilidae in five genera have been recorded in the islands. This is nearly one-third of the total number of known drosophilid species in the world. Their diversity of form, ecology, and behavior far exceeds the range of known variations in the group outside of Hawai'i.

Yet geneticists were astonished at how closely related many of these species are. Hampton Carson of the University of Hawaii has been able to trace changes in the banding patterns of the chromosomes among different species and to construct their family tree, thereby demonstrating the effects of founding new populations. More recently, Kenneth Kaneshiro of the Hawaiian Drosophila Project and the Hawaiian Evolutionary Biology Program (University of Hawaii) has been unraveling their courtship behavior and showing how the choice of a mate by the female plays an important role in the formation of new species.

The Hawaiian drosophilids

Table 2. *Genera of Hawaiian arthropods with 25 or more endemic species.*

Order: Family	Genus	No. of endemic species
Araneae: Tetragnathidae	*Tetragnatha*	(58)[1]
Odonata: Coenagrionidae	*Megalagrion*	30
Orthoptera: Gryllidae	Trigonidiinae (3 genera)	(150)
Psocoptera: Psocidae	*Ptycta*	61
Heteroptera: Miridae	*Nesiomiris*	(50)
Heteroptera: Nabidae	*Nabis*	30
Heteroptera: Lygaeidae	*Neseis*	38
Heteroptera: Lygaeidae	*Nysius*	27
Heteroptera: Lygaeidae	*Oceanides*	27
Homoptera: Cicadellidae	*Nesophrosyne*	63
Homoptera: Cixiidae	*Oliarus*	79
Homoptera: Delphacidae	*Nesosydne*	84
Coleoptera: Carabidae	*Mecyclothorax*	86
Coleoptera: Carabidae	*Metromenus*	27
Coleoptera: Histeridae	*Aeletes*	35
Coleoptera: Staphylinidae	*Diestota*	30
Coleoptera: Staphylinidae	*Oligota*	29
Coleoptera: Ciidae	*Cis*	34
Coleoptera: Elateridae	*Eopenthes*	33
Coleoptera: Eucnemidae	*Dromaeolus*	33
Coleoptera: Nitidulidae	*Eupetinus*	30
Coleoptera: Nitidulidae	*Nesopeplus*	31
Coleoptera: Nitidulidae	*Nesopetinus*	25
Coleoptera: Anobiidae	*Mirosternus*	71
Coleoptera: Anobiidae	*Xyletobius*	72
Coleoptera: Cerambycidae	*Plagithmysus*	139
Coleoptera: Aglycyderidae	*Proterhinus*	174
Coleoptera: Curculionidae	*Oodemas*	62
Coleoptera: Curculionidae	*Rhyncogonus*	34
Lepidoptera: Gracillariidae	*Philodoria*	30
Lepidoptera: Carposinidae	*Carposina*	49
Lepidoptera: Oecophoridae	*Thyrocopa*	40
Lepidoptera: Cosmopterigidae	*Hyposmocoma*	350
Lepidoptera: Crambidae	*Eudonia*	62
Lepidoptera: Crambidae	*Mestolobes*	33
Lepidoptera: Crambidae	*Udea*	45
Lepidoptera: Geometridae	*Scotorythra*	38
Lepidoptera: Noctuidae	*Agrotis*	26
Diptera: Dolichopodidae	*Campsicnemus*	137
Diptera: Dolichopodidae	*Eurynogaster*	56
Diptera: Pipunculidae	*Pipunculus*	38
Diptera: Drosophilidae	*Drosophila*	(600)
Diptera: Drosophilidae	*Scaptomyza*	(260)
Diptera: Muscidae	*Lispocephala*	103
Diptera: Calliphoridae	*Dyscritomyia*	26
Hymenoptera: Eupelmidae	*Eupelmus*	56
Hymenoptera: Bethylidae	*Sierola*	180
Hymenoptera: Vespidae	*Odynerus*	100
Hymenoptera: Colletidae	*Hylaeus*	64

[1] Parentheses include new species being described.

have been the most studied, but other native groups offer similar opportunities. For example, species of the native cutworms, *Agrotis* and *Peridroma*, and the corn earworm complex, *Helicoverpa*, represent valuable resources in applied evolutionary biology. Since each of these groups is closely related to important continental pest species, there is an opportunity for research on genetic controls. Such a project is now under way with the corn earworm complex.

Most native groups include both widespread successful species and rare, locally distributed species. These would be good candidate groups for determining the comparative ecological genetics of rarity and extinction. The 22 closely related spe-

cies in the pyralid moth genus *Omiodes* range from endemic agricultural pests (the sugarcane and coconut leaf rollers) to endangered or extinct species.

PREDATORY CATERPILLARS

One of the most remarkable adaptive shifts, the development of carnivorousness in moth caterpillars in the genus *Eupithecia*, was only recently discovered. In 1972, while admiring an extremely rare Hawai-

*This brown caterpillar (**Eupithecia** species A) hangs on a silken safety line.* ▶

In a turnabout, a predatory dolichopodid fly is captured and eaten by an inchworm (**Eupithecia niphoreas**). ▼

ian tree-like lobelia (*Delissea*), Steve Montgomery found a slender green inchworm eating a large fly and brought the larva back to the laboratory to rear and identify. Of course, everyone knows that caterpillars eat green leaves and other plant material and could not catch a live fly in any case, but this larva just sat on the lobelia leaf edge, waiting for days beyond what a normal plant-feeding larva could survive. Recalling his initial observation, Steve then added a fly to the cage, and the caterpillar caught it and ate it!

The ihchworm was a sit-and-wait predator, the first known example of ambush predation among moth and butterfly caterpillars. Extensive field work has shown that this adaptive shift led to a radiation of at least 18 distinct species using different types of perch sites (see Figures 125 to 140).

There are green caterpillars sitting on leaf margins and ferns; brown, wrinkled ones and spiny ones sitting on appropriately ornamented twigs; and some with moss-like tubercles perch on tree trunks amid moss. One living on ferns even modifies its perch: it chews out a gap between two leaflets so that it can hold onto the midrib and fit cryptically into the chewed-out notch. Then it captures insects walking along both the upper and lower surfaces of the midrib.

LIFE IN HAWAIIAN CAVES

It has long been assumed that young oceanic islands like the Big Island had many empty ecological

niches (i.e., food resources and habitats not fully exploited by native species), but recent evidence suggests that adaptive radiation may fill the available niches within a short time, like succession, rather than in the much longer evolutionary time. For example, it was thought that blind, white, specialized cave animals could not evolve on young volcanic islands like the Big Island.

There were four main reasons for this assumption: (1) lava tubes usually persist for only a few thousand years, a much shorter time than limestone caves where a specialized fauna has long been known; (2) moisture-loving animals that colonized continental caves did not disperse to Hawai'i; (3) important food resources in continental caves (stream debris and cave-roosting bats and birds) are absent from Hawaiian caves; and (4) such extreme physical changes displayed by cave species were assumed to take a long time, much longer than the age of the Big Island. However, one should assume nothing in science but test every hypothesis.

In 1971, Francis Howarth started working in Hawaiian lava tubes and found that they often supported a whole community of specialized cave animals. Many, such as lycosid spiders, *Thaumatogryllus* and *Caconemobius* crickets, *Nesidiolestes* bugs, and *Oliarus* planthoppers, represent the epitome of rapid morphological change associated with adaptive shifts. Indeed, one could say that the Hawaiian cave fauna contains ex-

Lava tubes are dark, foreboding places and, until recently, were thought to be devoid of life. In fact, many Hawaiian caves harbor diverse communities of specialized underground animals. Unfortunately, these communities are vulnerable both to human disturbance in the cave and to destruction of the vegetation on the surface above the cave.

amples of macro-evolution on micro-continents in mini-time. Also, many of these specialized cave animals are sensitive to human disturbance. Visitors may break plant roots, trample animals and their food and hiding places, and bring in pollutants.

Species in the cricket genus *Caconemobius* show clearly the separate stages of inter-island dispersal, colonization, adaptive shifts, and adaptive radiation (see Figures 43–47). All known species are wingless, mute, and adapted to foraging among bare wet rocks. A marine littoral species scavenges among large boulders in the wave-splashed zone on the shores of all the main islands. Since it lives in and can tolerate salt water, it has been able to disperse among the islands. On at least four islands, an adaptive shift to freshwater habitats has occurred. Kaua'i and Moloka'i each has a single, rare, big-eyed, black, nocturnal species living on wet cliffs in the mountains. Two pale, blind cave species live in lava tubes on Maui. But the youngest island, the Big Island, harbors the most surprising radiation. There, at least three cave species have evolved. They often live together in the same lava tubes but behave differently and show different degrees of cave adaptation. Surprisingly, crickets in one cave differ consistently from crickets of apparently the same species in other caves. We may be studying them during the process of divergence, perhaps just as new species are forming.

Closely related to these cave species is a remarkable black, big-eyed surface species, *Caconemobius fori*. Discovered in 1973, these crickets have adapted to living only on young, unvegetated lava flows on Kīlauea. They hide during the day deep in cracks and fumaroles and come out at night to feed on wind-borne debris, which can be quite abundant on these windy flows. These crickets move onto a new flow within a month after the surface cools, even when it is still warm. When plants start to colonize the flow, sometimes within 20 years, these crickets will move on to younger flows or die out.

Imagine the number of biologists who have stood near the sulfurous fumes at Kīlauea and perhaps even kicked a rock into the main vent at Halema'uma'u, saying, "Nothing could possibly live here." If they had looked more closely under that rock, they might have seen a cricket, lycosid spider, or some other animal that had adapted to that harsh environment.

Most biologists still assume that plants must colonize newly exposed land first, to provide food and cover for animals. In reality, animals usually arrive much sooner and may even aid the subsequent establishment of plants!

FLIGHTLESSNESS

A conspicuous theme among island insects is the evolution of flightlessness, and the Hawaiian

*An adult female Big Island cave cricket (**Caconemobius varius**) displays the reduced pigment, small eyes, and translucent exoskeleton that characterize cave animals. It probably evolved within the past 100,000 years from a dark, big-eyed, surface-dwelling ancestor much like the lava flow cricket (**C. fori**).*

fauna contains some of the best examples: flightless lacewings, moths, beetles, bugs, planthoppers, leafhoppers, crickets, katydids, wasps, and even flightless flies. In fact, of the 11 orders of insects that arrived in the islands with wings, only one, the Odonata (dragonflies and damselflies), has not evolved flightless species.

Flightlessness is not unique to islands or wind-swept, harsh environments but is common in every ecosystem. In fact, most resource exploitation is carried out by flightless organisms. Furthermore, nearly all insects spend the majority of their active lives in flightless stages. Consider the ants, termites, cockroaches, scales, springtails, and silverfish of homes and gardens.

Since most of the dominant flightless continental groups did not disperse to Hawai'i, many of the winged native Hawaiian species have evolved to fill these roles. What makes this process exciting in Hawai'i is that closely related flighted and flightless species often live side by side, and, sometimes, intermediate forms are still extant. Thus, in Hawai'i, the pieces of such interesting evolutionary puzzles as the development of flightlessness can be fitted together.

*The dark lava flow cricket (**Caconemobius fori**) lives only on very young barren lava flows on Kīlauea. It hides deep in moist cracks during the day and comes out at night to feed on material blown in by the wind.*

CONSERVATION

The Hawaiian fauna is in transition and profound changes are occurring. Many native groups are declining from the combined impacts of invasive alien organisms and the alteration of habitats resulting from the effects of human use and abuse of natural resources. These effects are compounded by the lack of knowledge of the status and biology of both native and alien species.

INVASIVE ALIEN SPECIES

Increasing contact with the outside world has broken the splendid isolation that allowed for the evolution of native island species. Invasive alien species, including plants, vertebrates, invertebrates, and microorganisms, are the most insidious and pervasive environmental threats. These species do not respect boundaries but invade all suitable habitats to which they can disperse. They are also virtually impossible to eradicate. Both intentionally and inadvertently introduced foreign species can now be found in virtually all habitats, from sea level to the summits of the highest mountains, where they compete with, prey on, parasitize, spread

The **koa** *bug* **Coleotichus blackburniae:** *the largest and most conspicuous native true bug.*

diseases among, or destroy the habitats of native organisms. Cows, goats, and other mammals continue to destroy the Hawaiian biota and "pasturize" its forests. The extinction of much of the native biota of Laysan Island after the introduction of rabbits in 1903 remains one of the clearest examples of the bad effects of alien species on an island ecosystem.

Even apparently innocuous alien species may be food for alien predators, reservoirs for diseases, pollinators for alien weeds, or dispersal agents for other alien species, thereby keeping their associated alien populations higher, which may inflict greater injury on native species. With the introduction of each new alien, the chance of its associated biota becoming established increases, which further decreases the prosperity of native species. About 3,260 species of alien arthropods have been either intentionally or unintentionally introduced to Hawai'i. Some populations have subsequently died out for the same reasons that some native populations are declining. Currently, there may be 2,500 species of alien arthropods successfully established. Ants with large aggressive colonies, such as the big-headed ant (*Pheidole megacephala*), Argentine ant (*Iridomyrmex humilis*), and long-legged ant (*Anoplolepis longipes*), have been strongly implicated in the extinction of many native species. In 1977, an aggressive race of the yellowjacket (*Vespula pensylvanica*) became established in Hawai'i, most likely through the importation of untreated Christmas trees. Its phenomenal population explosion and spread corresponded with an alarming decline in many native arthropods and possibly even some native birds.

ALTERATION OF HABITATS

Land conversion for agriculture, housing, and recreation was started by the early Hawaiians. Today, this is still occurring, often with devastating effects on the native biota. Fire, wood chipping for biomass energy and pressed board manufacture, silviculture, mining, pollution, military bombing and resultant fires, geothermal development, and powerline construction all have had major destructive effects on native habitats and the resident native species. Some prime native habitats have recently been cleared for dubious economic reasons. The freshwater aquatic fauna is being affected by stream channelization, impoundments, diversion, pollution, and alien species. The last includes introductions for control of mosquitoes and snails, as well as escapees from the aquarium trade.

Many Hawaiian insects are extremely host specific, with some groups of related species (for example, *Drosophila, Plagithmysus,* and *Nesiomiris*) even dividing up the resources of a single host species. Many Hawaiian species are confined to a very small area (for example, *Adelocosa anops, Rhynchogonus giffardi,* and *Rhynchogonus simplex*). The total known range of some *Prognathogryl-*

lus cricket species is less than a few acres. As their host plants become rarer and more scattered, or as their habitats shrink, these species become more vulnerable to extinction.

It is with mixed feelings that we call attention to the Hawaiian cave fauna, for the increase in public curiosity may lead to many more cave visitations. Caves, like bogs and sand dunes, are vulnerable to trampling and physical disturbances. In perhaps no other habitat are humans more intrusive than in the subterranean world of caves. Yet, there is a dilemma: If the existence of these remarkable cave animals is not made public, then their habitats may inadvertently be destroyed through ignorance during changes in land use on the surface over the caves. Had the cave fauna not been discovered, biologists would have continued to believe that no such fauna could ever have evolved in the islands.

LACK OF KNOWLEDGE OF NATIVE SPECIES

A serious obstacle to conserving Hawaiian insects is our lack of basic information on their status and biology. Furthermore, very few people are trained to obtain and disseminate this knowledge. We have not even given names to perhaps half the native species of insects. Without correct names and an understanding of the evolutionary relationships among species, other biological studies—including conservation biology—are impeded. Whether a population under study represents an alien or endemic species, or whether the population represents one or 10 or 100 closely related spe-

*This flightless weevil species (**Rhynchogonus simplex***) lives on less than an acre of land on O'ahu.*

cies, all have a direct bearing on the appropriateness of conservation programs. Some Hawaiian insect groups are so poorly known that they currently cannot be identified; thus, their management is largely ignored. Many native arthropods may become extinct without any documentation that they ever existed.

In nearly every native group that has been studied using modern methods, new species have been recognized. The best example is clearly the *Drosophila*, in which the number of known endemic species has risen from 48 in 1948 to over 600 under the University of Hawaii Drosophila Project. R.C.L. Perkins, during his survey for *Fauna Hawaiiensis*, never had a chance to collect moths and some other invertebrate groups on West Maui, nor in certain districts of the other islands. Based on the distribution of known species of the endemic moth genus *Hyposmocoma*, at least 80 new species in this genus are presumed to live on West Maui alone. A surprisingly large percentage of the species of arthropods illustrated in this book are not yet formally described, underscoring the need for biological surveys and related research programs.

CONSERVATION PROGRAMS

In spite of the threats facing the native Hawaiian biota, recent surveys confirm the existence of an abundance of native species that are worth saving. In fact, many large tracts of near-pristine ecosystems still exist, and good examples of most of the Hawaiian ecosystems can still be found, even in the lowlands. The islands continue to be important natural laboratories for studies in evolution, ecology, and conservation biology. This conclusion is also emphasized by recent discoveries, includ-

ing new species, new behaviors (for example, carnivorous caterpillars), and surprisingly new ecosystems in caves and on lava flows. Many equally incredible discoveries in island biology await the astute observer. As demonstrated in young Hawaiian caves and on the cold, stone desert on Mauna Kea, one must actually search all potential habitats for native species before writing these areas off as devoid of life.

Native Hawaiian species are vulnerable to pressures placed on them by alien species, but they are not inherently fragile. Recent conservation efforts have clearly demonstrated that native species respond remarkably well to appropriate management actions, and endangered species do recover. Species diversity in Hawai'i is so high that conservation efforts in selected areas will save many endangered species. Equally important for conservation biologists is to keep the common native species common so that they can be enjoyed by students and the public.

Effective conservation biology activities include establishing new research and education programs; setting up reserves with appropriate management; instituting legal and legislative support; improving quarantine programs along with stronger review procedures for screening proposed species introductions; and using more environmentally sound pest control programs. Long-term monitoring programs and ecological studies are needed to separate population fluctuations from irreversible changes, to assess the impacts of aliens, and to develop effective conservation measures. There has been a revival of interest in nature and the native plants and animals of Hawai'i. The major Hawaiian institutions currently encouraging and supporting research on and conservation of the native Hawaiian arthropods are the Bishop Museum, University of Hawaii, Hawaii Evolutionary Biology Program, Nature Conservancy of Hawaii, Hawaii Department of Land and Natural Resources, the United States National Park Service, and the United States Fish and Wildlife Service. In addition, a steady stream of biologists come to the islands from all over the world to conduct research in what they recognize as one of the most exciting natural laboratories anywhere.

'Ōla'a *rain forest epiphytes are being protected in Hawaii Volcanoes National Park.* ▶

Pelekunu Valley on Moloka'i is protected by the Nature Conservancy of Hawaii. ▼

INSECTS AS AN EDUCATIONAL RESOURCE

If insect conservation measures are to succeed, there must be greater public support. To that end, we need education programs that overcome people's fear of insects and instill an appreciation of the value and importance of insects and other invertebrates to human welfare.

Children have a natural curiosity about insects that can be focused to reinforce biological concepts, especially since insects and their relatives are ideal animals to keep and observe in the classroom. They are abundant and diverse; a great insect zoo exists near every school. Although many of the more conspicuous species in urban areas and near schools in Hawai'i are alien and harmful to the natural environment, even the worst of them can be used as good examples in lessons on how insects affect our lives and the Hawaiian Islands. These examples lead logically to lessons on nature conservation and the importance of good quarantines to protect the well-being of both native species and humans.

Insects dominate nearly all terrestrial and freshwater ecosystems; in fact, three-quarters of all living species are insects. Thus we increase our understanding of the world around us by understanding insect ways. Some are harmful to human endeavors, eating our crops, our homes, or our clothes. Some bite, sting, or spread diseases; others are nuisances. But the vast majority are beneficial, adding beauty to nature, cleaning up our waste, eating harmful pests, pollinating our crops, or, through our study of them, providing clues to evolution and ecology—the very secrets of life. The *Hawai'i Nature Study Program Guide on Insects* by Demanche and Hapai provides many interesting and useful activities for the classroom. Also, the Hawaii Nature Center, the Conservation Council of Hawaii, Bishop Museum, the Hawaii Department of Land and Natural Resources, the Hawaii Audubon Society, the National Audubon Society, and other local environmental groups produce and distribute educational materials on Hawaiian natural history.

QUESTIONS

Questions that can be used in the classroom include:
* How many kinds of insects live in the schoolyard, in houses, in parks, or in other habitats?

This colorful larva of an **Anomalochrysa** *species was found on an* **'ōhi'a lehua** *on Kaua'i.*

- How do insects affect the environment and humans?
- How much and what do different insects eat?
- How do they hide, eat, or behave?
- What do their eggs and young look like?
- How long does it take for an insect to grow up?
- How do the different life stages (life cycles) differ?
- What are the functions of the various insect structures, and how do these structures work?
- How do insects walk, crawl, swim, or fly?

KEEPING INSECTS

Insects and other arthropods are masters of disguise and camouflage. For example, the oleander sphinx caterpillar rears up and displays large blue "eye spots" that change an otherwise beautifully camouflaged green larva into an imposing big-eyed sphinx.

Searching for insects can be half the fun when studying them. They are everywhere, but it may take some ingenuity to find them. Look for them on flowers, fruits, and other potential foods; search in hiding places such as under bark or wooden, metallic, or plastic sheets on the ground. Baits, such as ripe fruits, host plants, and kitchen scraps, can be strategically placed and checked regularly. Many nocturnal insects are attracted to bright lights. A large

Deserts, dry forests, and rain forests can be adjacent to one another, as seen here on Kaua'i.

plastic sheet can be spread under a shrub or tree and the plant shaken to dislodge animals onto the sheet, where they are more easily seen. Or, leaf litter can be scattered onto the plastic sheet and the arthropods captured as they try to scurry off. An insect net works best for catching flying insects.

Cages can be made from large, wide-mouth glass or plastic containers (such as mayonnaise jars); punch holes in the lid or cover the mouth with netting. A clear plastic bottle can also be used by cutting off both ends, reinforcing the rims with stiff wire hoops, and covering the openings with netting held in place with rubber bands or tape. Crumpled paper, sand, or natural material can be added to provide the insect with better footing than bare glass or plastic. Fresh food should always be accessible in the cage. For plant-eating species, fresh cuttings of the host plant can be added regularly, or the open end of the bottle can be inverted directly over a potted plant and the insects observed on it. Water can be most easily provided by filling up a vial, plugging it with an absorbent cotton plug, and securing it in the cage so that the insect has access to moisture. Make sure the vial does not leak and drown the insect or roll around and injure it.

Any local species can be kept, although some experimentation will be necessary until the appropriate food and individual needs of the species are found. The food plants and basic biologies of many common species remain completely unknown, and their discovery would provide appropriate and valuable science fair projects for interested students. Most strong-flying insects, like moths, butterflies, and dragonflies, can be easily kept when they are young, but the adults need more space and do not do well in captivity. After the young emerge as adults and are studied, they can be released or preserved for future study. Some large moths and butterflies common in Hawaiian schoolyards are listed together with their preferred host plants in Table 3.

Table 3. *Some easily reared and observed moths and butterflies common in schoolyards in Hawai'i and suitable for classroom projects.*

Common name	Scientific name	Preferred food of caterpillars
MOTHS		
Oleander hawk moth	*Daphnis nerii*	oleander
Sweet potato hornworm	*Agrius cingulata*	morning glories
Maile pilau hornworm	*Macroglossum pyrrhostictum*	*maile pilau (Paederia foetida)*
Black witch	*Ascalapha odorata*	monkey pod tree
Croton caterpillar	*Achaea janata*	ornamental shrubs, mostly legumes and euphorbias
Koa haole moth	*Semiothisa abydata*	*koa haole (Leucaena)*
BUTTERFLIES		
Monarch	*Danaus plexippus*	milkweed and crown flower
Imported cabbageworm	*Pieris rapae*	cabbage family and nasturtium
Passion vine butterfly	*Agraulis vanillae*	passion vine *(Passiflora foetida)*
Citrus swallowtail	*Papilio xuthus*	citrus, esp. young leaves
Kamehameha butterfly	*Vanessa tameamea*	*mamaki (Pipturus)*
Blackburn butterfly	*Udara blackburni*	*koa* flowers, buds, and young leaves

THE NATIVE HAWAIIAN LAND ARTHROPODS

This overview draws on the excellent accounts in the *Insects of Hawaii* volumes and on a list of Hawaiian arthropods being prepared by Gordon Nishida, Scott Miller, Al Samuelson, and others at the Bishop Museum. A provisional summary of native and foreign arthropods in Hawai'i is listed in Table 1. It is sometimes difficult to determine whether a species is native, especially if it has no known close relatives in Hawai'i or if its group is poorly known in Hawai'i and neighboring tropical areas. This is especially true of the arachnids in general and mites (Acari) in particular. As the thousands of expected new species of native arthropods are discovered and described, our understanding of their classification and origins will improve. Also, significant discoveries are still being made in Hawaiian natural history. Even representatives of new groups continue to be discovered, thus increasing the number of presumed colonists to the islands.

Much new information has become available since Zimmerman published the introduction to *Insects of Hawaii* in 1948. Many new species have been described, new native

groups discovered, and some species thought to be native have been found elsewhere. However, Zimmerman's main theses—that the Hawaiian insect fauna is rich in species and that these evolved from a few original colonists—remain valid. What Hawai'i lacks in number of ancestral colonists it more than makes up for in number of species, for many native groups have undergone explosive radiation.

PHYLUM ARTHROPODA (ARTHROPODS)

The arthropods are animals without backbones, but with at least a partly segmented body and stiff external skeleton. They characteristically also have jointed legs and other appendages. This is by far the largest group of organisms, with more species than all other groups combined both in Hawai'i and in the world. This phylum is divided into several classes, five of which contain native terrestrial species that are included here.

Class Arachnida: spiders, mites, scorpions, and relatives. Excluding the Acari (mites), about 186 families of terrestrial arachnids are placed in 10 orders. Of these, only two orders and

A lush native ground cover grows in the Alaka'i Swamp on Kaua'i.

about 15 families occur naturally in Hawai'i.

Order Pseudoscorpiones: false scorpions. Ten species are recorded from Hawai'i, but, except for three endemic cave species in *Tyrannochthonius*, their status is unknown. Pseudoscorpions that are associated with sea birds' nests should have been early arrivals in Hawai'i; it is surprising that they have not speciated more extensively. Specific collecting will certainly increase the number of known species.

Order Acari: mites and ticks. Mites remain so poorly known that it is difficult to determine whether or not a given species is native. About 500 species are recorded from Hawai'i, of which 100 are considered native. But these numbers will change significantly as the mites become better known.

Order Araneae: spiders. Hawaiian spiders remain poorly known, and many new species remain to be discovered. Most species are nocturnal and often escape the notice of insect collectors. Currently, only 10 of the 105 recognized spider families have native representatives; another six families are doubtful, each being represented by a single questionably endemic species (see Table 4). About 30 separate colonists can account for the presently recognized native spider fauna, but this number will surely rise as more native groups are discovered. Most of the native spiders belong to groups that disperse by ballooning or hang-gliding—that is, the spiderlings release into the wind enough silk to allow them to be carried aloft. Some, like the lycosid wolf spiders, are such efficient hang-gliders that they are among the first organisms to colonize new islands and habitats; and Hawaiian species have made surprising adaptive shifts to colonize caves and new lava flows. The desids live along sea coasts and could have been dispersed by rafting on ocean currents.

A few groups have undergone extensive adaptive radiation, with

Table 4. *Families of spiders (Araneae) with native species in Hawai'i.*

Family	Common name	No. of native genera	No. of native species
Barychelidae[1]	barychelid spiders	1	1
Oonopidae	oonopid spiders	6	8
Anapidae[1]	anapid spiders	1	1
Ochyroceratidae[1]	ochyroceratid spiders	1	1
Segestriidae[1]	segestriid spiders	1	1
Theridiidae	comb-footed spiders	4	15
Linyphiidae	sheet web spiders	6	7
Araneidae	orb web spiders	2	8
Tetragnathidae	long-jawed spiders	2	(59)[2]
Desidae	sea shore spiders	1	1
Zodariidae[1]	zodariid spiders	1	1
Lycosidae	wolf spiders	4	12
Gnaphosidae[1]	hunting spiders	1	1
Thomisidae	crab spiders	3	21
Philodromidae	crab spiders	2	9
Salticidae	jumping spiders	1	8

[1] Questionably native species.
[2] Parentheses include new species being described.

large numbers of diverse but closely related species. The most conspicuous of these is found among the long-jawed spiders (Tetragnathidae); these are being studied by Rosemary Gillespie (University of Hawaii, Zoology Department), who has discovered some 50 new species. The Hawaiian tetragnathids far exceed the limits of form and behavior of the group outside of Hawai'i. The sheet-web spiders (Linyphiidae) are also more diverse than currently recognized. They live from the sea coast to rain forests. Three species even live under stones at the frozen summit of Mauna Kea. Blind species live in caves, and some are so unusual it is hard to tell that they are linyphiids.

Class Crustacea: crabs, shrimps, barnacles, sowbugs, scuds, and relatives. Most crustaceans are aquatic. Only two orders have successfully invaded terrestrial habitats, and both contain native species.

Order Amphipoda: scuds, sandhoppers. Amphipods are almost entirely marine and freshwater, but one small family (Talitridae) has invaded terrestrial habitats, especially in the Southern Hemisphere and on islands. Hawai'i has an exceptionally diverse terrestrial amphipod fauna, with more than 30 endemic species, mostly undescribed, representing several separate radiations. The endemic terrestrial species live on all of the main islands except, surprisingly, the Big Island. They live in leaf litter, leaf axils, rotting wood, and mosses; and one (a remarkable, rare, blind species—*Spelaeorchestia koloana*) lives in caves on Kaua'i.

Order Isopoda: isopods, sowbugs, woodlice, pillbugs. Isopods inhabit mostly marine and fresh waters, but a large, diverse group lives on land.

About 40 species have been recorded from Hawai'i, but many more are already in collections. They live in leaf litter in most vegetated habitats and are sometimes abundant. The group is poorly known, but most species are considered alien. The native species inhabit the marine littoral zone, rain forests, and caves.

Class Diplopoda: millipedes. Millipedes are generally poorly represented on oceanic islands, but two families in two orders are native to Hawai'i. The genus *Nannolene* (formerly called *Dimerogonus*) in the family Camballidae, contains 15 described native species and at least two new blind ones from caves. The tiny bristly millipedes (3–7 mm long), family Polyxenidae, are not well known. But two species have been described from Hawai'i, and additional blind populations are known to live in caves. A few polyxenids elsewhere are salt tolerant and live along shores; thus, ancestors of the Hawaiian species could have come via the sea.

Class Chilopoda: centipedes. Only one group of centipedes contains native species. The rock centipedes (family Lithobiidae) apparently have many native and introduced species in Hawai'i, although only six are recorded. A tiny (1 cm in length) black species lives at the summit of Mauna Kea; larger, brown mottled species are common in rain forests; large, pale, blind species live in caves; and medium-sized species live in compost in disturbed areas. Most centipedes are small and cryptic, but the large, ominous, alien *Scolopendra subspinipes* reaches 12 cm in length and can inflict a painful bite.

Class Insecta: insects. Of the 34 currently recognized orders of insects,

16 are represented in the native fauna. Another 11 orders have been introduced by humans.

Order Collembola: springtails. The springtails are a large group of primitively wingless insects. Currently, 128 species are recorded from Hawai'i, of which about 50 are considered native. They occupy a wide range of habitats, mostly in soil and leaf litter, but some are arboreal. A few live in the cold desert at the summit of Mauna Kea. Several pale, blind species live in lava tubes. Some of the native terrestrial species evolved from marine littoral ancestors.

Order Microcoryphia: jumping bristletails. Native jumping bristletails in the genus *Machiloides* inhabit all the main islands, where they live in leaf litter and under loose bark in mesic, mid-elevation forests. They may have dispersed to Hawai'i via the sea and evolved from a marine littoral ancestor, since their closest known relative now lives along the southwestern shores of North America.

Order Odonata: damselflies and dragonflies. Only three of the 25 families of odonates occur naturally in Hawai'i: Coenagrionidae, Aeshnidae, and Libellulidae. *Megalagrion* damselflies (family Coenagrionidae)

◄ **Koa** *(Acacia koa) and* **'ie'ie** *(Freycinetia arborea) grow intertwined in mesic forests.*

Large areas of native forest with their insect faunas are found on O'ahu, for example along Poamoho Trail. ▼

are among the marvels of Hawaiian insects. The 30 presently known species probably evolved from a single ancestor, yet their diversity is surprising. The immature stages of the different species have adapted to a wide range of moist habitats, culminating in *Megalagrion oahuense*, one of the very few truly terrestrial damselflies in the world.

There are two endemic dragonflies: the giant aeshnid—*Anax strenuus*—the largest native insect with a 15-cm wingspan, and the libellulid *Nesogonia blackburni*. Two species of dragonflies are indigenous: the globe skimmer, *Pantala flavescens*, is regularly found flying over the Pacific far from land and probably infrequently disperses to and from Hawai'i; the green darner, *Anax junius*, is closely related to *Anax strenuus* and widely distributed over most of the Northern Hemisphere.

Order Orthoptera: grasshoppers, katydids, and crickets. Two families, the katydids (Tettigoniidae) and the crickets (Gryllidae), include native species. Another four families (Acrididae, Pyrgomorphidae, Tetrigidae, and Gryllotalpidae) are represented by more than 20 foreign species. The Hawaiian katydids represent two evolutionary lines in the Conocephalinae (cone-headed katydids): one possibly extinct endemic species in the widespread genus *Ruspolia* and 11 species in the endemic genus *Banza*. The native crickets are placed in eight genera in three subfamilies: *Caconemobius* and *Thetella* in the ground crickets (Nemobiinae); *Laupala*, *Prolaupala*, and *Anaxipha* in the sword-tail crickets (Trigonidiinae); and three closely related endemic genera (*Prognathogryllus*, *Leptogryllus*, and *Thaumatogryllus*) in the tree crickets (Oecanthinae). Studies now in pro-

gress, by Dan Otte (Philadelphia Academy of Science) and Robin Rice (University of Hawaii), will bring the number of named, endemic Hawaiian crickets to over 200 species, which is more than twice the total known for the continental United States.

Order Dermaptera: earwigs. Zimmerman considered all Hawaiian earwigs to be foreign, but *Anisolabis maritima* is a widespread marine littoral species that is indigenous. Multiple invasions by it, or more likely its ancestors, gave rise to a group of seven closely related endemic species, including the cave-adapted *Anisolabis howarthi*.

Order Psocoptera: barklice and booklice. The number of endemic species has more than tripled (from 24 to 75) since Zimmerman's 1948 account, but studies being done by Ian Thornton (LaTrobe University, Australia) will probably triple it again to over 200 species. The endemic species are placed in three genera belonging to two families (Psocidae and Elipsocidae). They are mostly scavengers and lichen feeders on woody vegetation and serve as important food for native birds and other insect-eaters. Many psocids are easily transported by the wind, and five widespread species are considered indigenous.

Order Mallophaga: chewing lice. The chewing lice are parasites of birds and mammals. Unfortunately, Perkins' collections for *Fauna Hawaiiensis* were lost; thus many native species associated with native birds became extinct with their hosts without becoming known to science. Fifteen indigenous species are associated with wide-ranging sea birds.

Order Thysanoptera: thrips. Thrips

are small insects (0.5–3 mm long) with a characteristically elongated shape. Most species suck sap from plants, but many are predaceous on insects and mites. Of the eight recognized families, two are native to Hawai'i. Two genera (*Hoplothrips* in the Phlaeothripidae with 13 species, and *Neurisothrips* in the Thripidae with seven species) have undergone small adaptive radiations in Hawai'i.

The elfin cloud forest along the crest of the Ko'olau Mountains on O'ahu supports many native plants and their associated insects.

Another six genera in the Phlaeothripidae are each represented by one or two apparently endemic species. Like psocids, thrips are small and easily transported by wind; thus, some of the listed alien species may in fact be indigenous.

Order Heteroptera: true bugs. The true bugs are a large and diverse order. Most feed on plants, but a large proportion are predaceous. Many are aquatic and a few groups are marine. Hawai'i has a relatively rich Heteroptera fauna. Of the approximately 60 families recognized, 13 or 14 have native species (see Table 5).

Several unusual adaptive shifts have occurred. The seed bug *Nysius wekiuicola* lives among loose volcanic cinders at the margins of snow banks on Mauna Kea. The thread-legged bug *Nesidiolestes ana* and the terrestrial water-treader *Speleovelia aaa* are blind and live in caves. The damsel bugs (*Nabis* species) are predaceous, but some endemic species hunt prey only on a single species of plant. Some predaceous mirid leaf bugs are also host specific. Such narrow specialization to a host plant is unusual among predatory insects. The most atypical damsel bug was only recently discovered; it hunts along stream margins, thus switching roles with several endemic shore bugs (*Saldula* species) that live in trees and leaf litter rather than along stream margins, like their relatives.

Many new species remain to be described, especially in the Miridae. Wayne Gagné of Bishop Museum had over 200 new species of mirids sorted for description before he suddenly passed away in 1988.

Order Homoptera: hoppers, whiteflies, aphids, and scale insects. The homopterans are all phytophagous and suck sap from plant tissue. The group is large and diverse; about 50 families are recognized, of which only six have endemic species (see Table 6). No species is currently thought to be indigenous, but the ease with which some aphids and other small homopterans are able to disperse in the wind suggests otherwise. Hawai'i is relatively rich in Homoptera species. The genera

Table 5. *Families of true bugs (Heteroptera) with native species in Hawai'i.*

Family	Common name	No. of native genera	No. of native species[1]
Enicocephalidae[2]	gnat bugs	1	1
Gerridae	water striders	1	2
Hermatobatidae	marine water striders	1	1
Mesoveliidae	water treaders	1	1
Veliidae	ripple bugs	1	1
Saldidae	shore bugs	1	8
Miridae	leaf bugs	14	(90)[3]
Reduviidae (Emesinae)	thread-legged bugs	2	7
Nabidae	damsel bugs	1	31
Anthocoridae	minute pirate bugs	2	6
Pentatomidae	stink bugs	1	14
Scutelleridae	shield-backed bugs	1	1
Lygaeidae	seed bugs	11	109
Rhopalidae	scentless plant bugs	1	2

[1] Includes both endemic and indigenous species.
[2] Questionably native species.
[3] Parentheses include new species being described.

Oliarus (Cixiidae) with 79-plus species, *Nesosydne* (Delphacidae) with 84 species, and *Nesophrosyne* (Cicadellidae) with 63 species represent classic examples of adaptive radiation. There are some spectacular developments among the native species. For example, delphacids in the endemic genus *Dictyophorodelphax* superficially resemble another planthopper family, the Dictyopharidae.

Recent electronic inventions allow the study of sounds made by insects that are normally inaudible to humans. These "songs" are transmitted through the substrate rather than through the air and are used by many insects to communicate, especially during courtship.

The study of these songs is revolutionizing our understanding of insect behavior and biology. The leafhoppers and planthoppers have a rich repertoire of substrate-borne songs, and studies being done by Hannelore Hoch and Manfred Asche (both of Marburg University, Germany) and associates are turning up some surprising results. The cave cixiid, *Oliarus polyphemus*, has a reduced song compared to some of its big-eyed, surface relatives, but each cave population sings its own unique song. Some songs are so distinct that the populations are probably separate species.

Order Neuroptera: lacewings and antlions. Neuropterans usually have four large, net-veined wings and are weak fliers. They prey on other insects. Around the world, there are 17 families in the order, three of which are represented in Hawai'i: the green lacewings (Chrysopidae, with 22 species); the brown lacewings (Hemerobiidae, with 26 species); and the antlions (Myrmeleonidae, with three species).

Hawaiian green lacewings, genus *Anomalochrysa*, are relatively large with a wingspan of up to nearly 5 cm. They are beautiful insects with green, brown, gray, or shades of red colors. One Maui species has maroon wings with a wide, silver stripe along

Looking down Kīpahulu Valley on East Maui from alpine shrub at 2,000 m (6,600 ft) to the sea. Large areas of near pristine habitats still exist and support hundreds of native arthropod species, many of which are still unknown to science. This valley is protected wilderness within the Haleakalā National Park.

Table 6. *Families of Homoptera (leafhoppers, planthoppers, psyllids, and scale insects) with native species in Hawai'i.*

Family	Common name	No. of native genera	No. of native species
Cicadellidae	leafhoppers	6	80
Cixiidae	cixiid planthoppers	2	88
Delphacidae	delphacid planthoppers	9	143
Psyllidae	psyllids	9	35
Pseudococcidae	mealybugs	12	30
Halimococcidae	palm scales	2	3

the anterior margins. The brown lacewings represent one of the more remarkable products of island evolution. Some, like *Nesomicromus paradoxus*, have bizarre wing shapes. The most unusual are the flightless, beetle-like species in *Pseudopsectra* and *Nesothauma*. Each of these five flightless species apparently evolved independently from separate ancestral endemic species of *Nesomicromus*.

Order Coleoptera: beetles. This is the largest order of animals, with over 290,000 species in 135 families worldwide. In Hawai'i, 1,355 species in 30 families are native (see Table 7). Seven families have undergone extensive adaptive radiation and contain the bulk of the native species. The 229 species of ground beetles, Carabidae, prey on other invertebrates. They live in most habitats but are most diverse in rain forests.

Of the three native genera of long-horned woodborers (Cerambycidae), why the endemic genus *Plagithmysus* has radiated so dramatically while the other two native genera have only one endemic species each has long intrigued evolutionary biologists. *Plagithmysus* attacks living plants, and each species has a narrow host range, perhaps specializing to cope with its host's defenses. *Parandra* and *Megopis*, in contrast, bore in dead wood and have broad host ranges.

The 174 species of endemic *Proterhinus* represent all but a few of the world's fauna of primitive weevils, Aglycyderidae. The true weevils, Curculionidae, are popular among insect collectors and are relatively well known; yet new species of even the showy *Rhynchogonus* continue to be found. Some adult *Achalles* weevils hide themselves by using a mutually beneficial relationship with living colonies of algae and fungi that grow on their bodies.

More than 600 alien species of beetles are now found in Hawai'i. Some, such as many scarabs and lady beetles, were purposely introduced for biological control. A few alien beetles are serious pests. The inadvertently introduced black twig borer, *Xylosandrus compactus*, damages a wide range of both commercial and native plants.

Order Lepidoptera: moths and butterflies. About 950 species of native moths have been described in 17 families (see Table 8). In contrast, only two native butterflies in two families (Nymphalidae and Lycaenidae) are known. The 19 native families represent less than 20% of the families of Lepidoptera.

Most native moths are small, with a wingspan of less than 1 cm. Smaller insects disperse much more easily to islands than larger species do. Only a few large, showy Lepidoptera are native, and most of these

The native lowland dry forest has been severely reduced in area in recent times, but important examples of some larger tracts, such as here at Kanaio, Maui, remain relatively intact.

Table 7. *Families of beetles (Coleoptera) with native species in Hawai'i.*

Family	Common name	No. of native genera	No. of native species[1]
Carabidae	ground beetles	23	219
Dytiscidae	predaceous diving beetles	1	1
Histeridae	hister beetles	2	37
Hydrophilidae	water scavenger beetles	2	2
Ptiliidae	feather-winged beetles	1	5
Scaphidiidae	shining fungus beetles	1	1
Staphylinidae	rove beetles	17	100
Clambidae	fringe-winged beetles	1	1
Scydmaenidae	antlike stone beetles	1	1
Corylophidae	minute fungus beetles	5	8
Dermestidae	dermestid beetles	3	20
Ciidae	minute tree-fungus beetles	2	48
Elateridae	click beetles	5	45
Eucnemidae	false click beetles	2	34
Erotylidae	pleasing fungus beetles	1	1
Cucujidae	flat bark beetles	3	14
Nitidulidae	souring (or sap) beetles	13	144
Discolomidae	discolomid beetles	1	1
Jacobsoniidae	jacobsoniid beetles	1	1
Propalticidae	propalticid beetles	1	1
Colydiidae	cylindrical bark beetles	1	1
Tenebrionidae	darkling beetles	2	2
Alleculidae	comb-clawed beetles	2	10
Anobiidae	death-watch beetles	5	159
Lucanidae	stag beetles	1	1
Cerambycidae	long-horned wood borers	3	141
Anthribidae	fungus weevils	1	2
Scolytidae	bark beetles	2	20
Aglycyderidae	primitive weevils	1	174
Curculionidae	true weevils	16	167

[1] Includes both endemic and indigenous species.

Table 8. *Families of moths and butterflies (Lepidoptera) with native species in Hawai'i.*

Family	Common name	No. of native genera	No. of native species
Opostegidae	opostegid leaf miners	1	6
Tortricidae	leaf rollers	13	77
Gracillariidae	gracillariid leaf miners	1	30
Lyonetiidae	lyonetiid leaf miners	1	13
Yponomeutidae	yponomeutid fruit moths	1	7
Plutellidae	diamond-back moths	1	1
Acrolepiidae	acrolephiid leaf miners	1	4
Carposinidae	carposinid fruit moths	1	49
Oecophoridae	oecophoridae moths	1	40
Coleophoridae	coleophorid moths	1	6
Cosmopterigidae	cosmopterigid moths	2	355
Gelechiidae	gelechiid moths	1	21
Pyralidae	pyralid moths	4	6
Crambidae	crambid moths	11	197
Sphingidae	hawk moths	3	6
Geometridae	inchworms	7	73
Noctuidae	noctuid moths	13	74
Nymphalidae	brush-footed butterflies	1	1
Lycaenidae	blue butterflies	1	1

belong to groups noted for their migrations or strong flight. The hawk moths, the Kamehameha butterfly (*Vanessa tameamea*), and some noctuids are examples. On the other hand, some native moths display gigantism, being much larger than their relatives. *Thyrocopa gigas*, an oecophorid "micro moth," has a wingspan of over 5 cm.

The endemic genus *Hyposmocoma* (Cosmopterigidae), with 350 described species, comprises over one-third of the known native moth species. Their diversity of habit and form is truly remarkable. The adult forms are so diverse that these species were originally placed in 14 separate genera. Most of the larvae are scavengers or eat lichens on rocks and vegetation; many are wood borers; a few are aquatic. They live in areas from sea level to above tree line, from barren, dry lava flows to rain forests, and from near-pristine native forests to disturbed habitats.

Most native moth groups are poorly known. Even in *Hyposmocoma* at least 150 new species are expected. More than 100 species of *Eudonia* (Crambidae) are already in collec-

tions, but only 62 are described. The recent discovery of new species and predatory behavior in the *Eupithecia* larvae emphasizes the value of a biological survey. Many moth species appear to have become extinct since 1900, but a diverse native fauna still survives. Some *Hyposmocoma* species remain common even in urban Honolulu. Several native moths regularly gather around lights in the city, including *Mestolobes minuscula*, *Omiodes localis*, and four species of *Eudonia*. The common coconut leaf roller (*Omiodes blackburni*) and sugarcane leaf roller (*Omiodes accepta*) are endemic crambids.

Order Diptera: true flies. Over 1,100 species of flies belonging to 28 families are native to Hawai'i (see Table 9). The order may be better known than the others because of the labor

This mature rain forest patch on the Big Island is a **kīpuka** *(an island of older vegetation surrounded by younger lava flows).* **Kīpuka** *encapsulate patches of forest of different ages, thereby allowing comparative studies not only of succession on lava flows, but also of evolutionary phenomena on islands within islands.*

of D.E. Hardy and the activities of the Hawai'i Drosophila Project. Still, new species and discoveries continue to surprise entomologists. Even in the largest family, Drosophilidae, 200 undescribed species are already in collections and new ones continue to be found.

Dipterans are relatively well represented on islands. Wind probably brought most flies to Hawai'i. Even the gall midges, Cecidomyiidae, which appear to be such fragile flies, are easily transported in the wind, and the 16 endemic species represent about 11 separate colonizations. The Hawaiian Drosophilidae are thought to have evolved from only one or perhaps two separate colonizations. The louse flies

(Hippoboscidae) arrived with their bird hosts, and those on wide-ranging sea birds are indigenous. Dipterans are the best-represented freshwater aquatic group in the islands. Most of these freshwater flies are closely related to marine species and their ancestors probably arrived via the sea. The Tipulidae, Ceratopogonidae, Chironomidae, Empididae, Dolichopodidae, Ephydridae, Tethinidae, and Canacidae have species that appear to have made the adaptive shift from salt water to fresh water, and a few even occupy terrestrial habitats in Hawai'i.

In addition to the remarkable radiations of species evident (see Table 9), there have been numerous adaptive shifts and unusual evolu-

Table 9. *Families of true flies (Diptera) with native species in Hawai'i.*

Family	Common name	No. of native genera	No. of native species[1]
Tipulidae	crane flies	2	16
Psychodidae	moth flies	2	6
Chironomidae	non-biting midges	6	28
Ceratopogonidae	biting midges	2	7
Keroplatidae	fungus gnats	2	5
Sciaridae	dark-winged fungus gnats	8	14
Cecidomyiidae	gall midges	10	16
Empididae	dance flies	1	2
Dolichopodidae	long-legged flies	7	200
Phoridae	humpbacked flies	3	11
Pipunculidae	big-headed flies	1	38
Tephritidae	fruit flies	3	25
Sphaeroceridae	small dung flies	2	2
Chyromyidae	chyromyid flies	2	3
Agromyzidae	agromyzid leaf miners	2	2
Asteiidae	asteiid flies	3	11
Xenasteiidae[2]	xenasteiid flies	1	1
Stenomicridae[2]	stenomicrid flies	1	1
Ephydridae	shore flies	7	26
Drosophilidae	pomace flies	5	570
Milichiidae	milichiid flies	2	2
Tethinidae	tethinid beach flies	2	3
Canacidae	beach flies	2	11
Hippoboscidae	louse flies	3	4
Muscidae	house flies	2	105
Calliphoridae	blow flies	2	26

[1] Includes both endemic and indigenous species.
[2] Questionably native species.

tionary developments. The complex courtship behavior in *Drosophila*, which often includes the defense of a territory (*lek* site) by a male, is providing clues to Darwin's "mystery of mysteries"—the formation of new species. Crane flies normally have aquatic or semi-aquatic larvae, but one Hawaiian species, *Limonia kauaiensis*, is unique in the family in being a leaf miner. *Lispocephala* flies (Muscidae) are predators; in one group of species the adults are aquatic and have adapted to walking on rocks in swift streams where they prey on fly larvae. Adult native blow flies feed on protein-rich foods; some are possibly associated with native land snails. These flies have independently evolved the ability to nurture their larvae internally, giving birth to one nearly mature larva at a time. The tsetse flies of Africa and some others give birth to a single larva all ready to pupate and turn into an adult. *Dyscritomyia* species are intermediate and show how small changes can have big evolutionary consequences.

Order Siphonaptera: fleas. Fleas are all blood-sucking parasites of vertebrates. Only one endemic species is known, *Parapsyllus laysanensis* (Rhoparopsyllidae), which is associated with sea birds on the northwestern Hawaiian Islands.

Order Hymenoptera: bees, wasps, and ants. Hymenopterans are a large and diverse group. There are about 580 endemic wasps in 15 families and 64 endemic bees in one family (see Table 10). No species in the primitive suborder Symphyta, which feed mainly on plants, is native in Hawai'i. Also, no ants or any true social wasps or bees made it to Hawai'i without the aid of humans.

The native yellow-faced bees (Colletidae) are a remarkable assemblage and important pollinators of native plants. Some Hawaiian species have become kleptoparasitic, stealing or usurping nest provisions from more industrious related species and independently imitating the behavior of unrelated kleptoparasitic bees elsewhere.

Table 10. *Families of wasps and bees (Hymenoptera) with native species in Hawai'i.*

Family	Common name	No. of native genera	No. of native species[1]
Braconidae	braconid wasps	3	4
Ichneumonidae	ichneumon wasps	7	43
Mymaridae	fairyflies	2	17
Trichogrammatidae	trichogrammatid wasps	1	3
Eulophidae	eulophid wasps	4	10
Encyrtidae	encyrtid wasps	6	29
Eupelmidae	eupelmid wasps	2	59
Pteromalidae	pteromalid wasps	6	15
Eucoilidae	eucoilid wasps	11	44
Diapriidae	diapriid wasps	3	9
Scelionidae	scelionid wasps	3	9
Bethylidae	bethylid wasps	2	196
Dryinidae	dryinid wasps	1	1
Vespidae	potter wasps	4	116
Sphecidae	square-headed wasps	3	33
Colletidae	yellow-faced bees	1	64

[1] Includes both endemic and indigenous species.

Most native wasp species are parasites of other arthropods. Some species have a narrow host range; others attack a wide range of prey. Probably few native arthropods, including some wasps themselves, escape being parasitized by one or more species. Mymarids and trichogrammatids are among the tiniest of insects and parasitize insect eggs.

Most encyrtids attack scale insects. Eucoilids attack fly pupae. Adults of *Kleidotoma* (Eucoilidae) can walk on rocks under water, sometimes in swift moving streams, where they lay their eggs in the pupae of native canacid and ephydrid flies. Vespids and sphecids are predators. Each female provisions a burrow or nest with an immobilized prey upon which she places her eggs. Native vespids specialize in capturing Lepidoptera caterpillars. Most native sphecids capture adult flies.

The importance of the parasitic Hymenoptera in controlling the populations of many insects has long been recognized; over 240 species of alien wasps have been purposely introduced to Hawai'i for pest control. About 170 species have become established, providing many examples of successful control. An additional 400 species of wasps, including 50 ants, have been introduced inadvertently through human activity. The combined effect of all these foreign parasites and predators has been devastating to the native fauna, reducing populations and causing extinction of native species.

◄ *This rain forest patch on the Big Island was isolated by rugged lava flows and had escaped the ravages of introduced pigs and other larger mammals. It was like a lost world of unusually rich biological diversity.*

*The **Ka'ū** silversword occurs in open areas near the boundary between montane rain forest and alpine shrub on Mauna Loa on the Big Island. These silverswords support a unique native arthropod community whose members are closely related to species found in the silversword and greensword communities on Mauna Kea and Maui. Only a few small populations survive, and it is a clear candidate for endangered species status. As the silversword populations decline, the associated community will become more impoverished.* ▼

INSECTS AND THEIR KIN

1▲   2▼

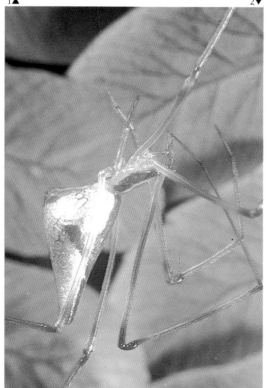

PSEUDOSCORPIONES

1. *Pseudoscorpiones (Endemic? All islands? Predator). An unknown female tends her eggs under bark in an upper montane Big Island rain forest.*

SPIDERS

2. **Ariamnes** *(Theridiidae. Endemic. Kaua'i. Wet forests. Predator). These spiders hang upside-down from small webs under living leaves. Similar species live on other islands.*

3. **Theridion grallator** *(Theridiidae. Happyface spider. Endemic. O'ahu to Big Island. Rain forests. Predator). Female from O'ahu tends her eggs. Females guard their eggs and capture prey for their young until the spiderlings are old enough to disperse and fend for themselves.*

(Page 58) **Vanessa tameamea** *male.*

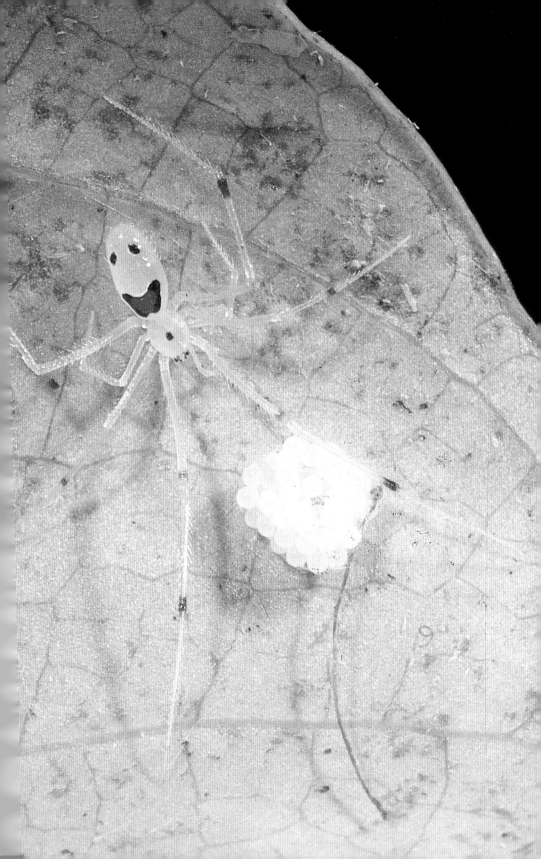

4. **Theridion grallator** (*Theridiidae. Happyface spider. Endemic. O'ahu to Big Island. Rain forests. Predator*). *Male from Big Island. The variation in color pattern among different populations of this species is surprising.*

5. **Theridion grallator**. *Female happyface from the Big Island showing another of the many different designs known.*

6. **Argiope appensa** (*Araneidae. A garden spider. Foreign. Kaua'i to Big Island. Lowland habitats. Predator*). *An adult female on her typical orb web eating a honey bee (**Apis mellifera**) while a smaller male spider waits nearby.*

5▲

6▼

7. **Tetragnatha brevignatha** (*Male.*
Tetragnathidae. Green, spiny-legged, long-jawed
spider. Endemic. Big Island. Rain forests.
Predator). Unlike others outside of Hawai'i, this
and several related species do not build an orb
web but actively hunt down prey instead.

8. **Tetragnatha quasimodo** (*Female.*
Tetragnathidae. Humpbacked, spiny-legged,
long-jawed spider. Endemic. Big Island. Rain
forests. Predator). This spider belongs to one of
more than 50 recently discovered species.

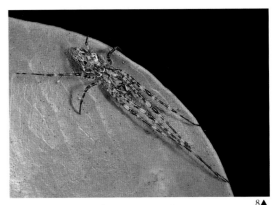

9. **Lycosa** species (*Lycosidae. Lava flow hunting*
spider. Unidentified. Endemic. Big Island.
Montane ecosystems on lava flows. Predator).
Wolf spider females care for their eggs and
young. Surface lycosids, like this species, often
have over 300 spiderlings per clutch, which stay
with their mother for at least a month. The empty
egg sac is under the female.

10. **Lycosa howarthi** (*Lycosidae. Small-eyed,*
big-eyed hunting spider. Endemic. Big Island.
Lava tubes). This intermediate cave-adapted
species has about 40 spiderlings per clutch,
which stay with their mother for about two
weeks.

8▲

10▼ 9▲

11▲

12▲

11. **Adelocosa anops** (Lycosidae. No-eyed, big-eyed hunting spider. Endemic. Kaua'i. Very rare. Lava tubes. Predator). *These have about 25 young per clutch, which remain with the mother only a few days. Note the size of the spiderlings compared to those of* **Lycosa howarthi** *and especially those of* **Lycosa** *species.*

12. **Heteropoda venatoria** (Sparassidae. Cane spider. Foreign. Kaua'i to Big Island. Lowland habitats. Predator). *This giant crab spider is common around houses, where it preys on cockroaches and other insects. Despite their imposing size (75 mm, 3-inch leg span), they are harmless to humans. Females, shown here, carry their egg sacs with their jaws.*

13. **Misumenops vitellinus**? (Thomisidae. Masked crab spider. Endemic. Kaua'i, O'ahu, Maui Nui, Big Island. Open and closed mid-elevation forests. Predator). *Crab spiders don't build webs but spin a dragline as they move about. This species ambushes prey on vegetation.*

14. **Misumenops** species (Thomisidae. Flower-dwelling crab spider. Unidentified. Endemic. Big Island. Rain forests. Predator). *This species ambushes insects visiting flowers.*

13▼

15. **Mecaphesa** *species A (Undescribed. Thomisidae. Moss crab spider. Endemic. Big Island. Very wet rain forests. Predator). This beautifully camouflaged female blends into mossy environments.*

16. **Mecaphesa** *species B (Undescribed. Male. Thomisidae. Long-legged moss crab spider. Endemic. O'ahu. Montane cloud forest bog. Predator). Known only from Mt. Ka'ala summit, O'ahu, where it mimics its mossy perch.*

SANDHOPPERS

17. **Spelaeorchestia koloana** *(Talitridae. Kaua'i cave amphipod. Endemic. Lava tubes and limestone caves. Feeds on plant roots and debris. Very rare). This translucent, blind, cave-adapted terrestrial amphipod lives only in a few caves on Kaua'i.*

18. **Platorchestia pickeringi** *(Talitridae. Ko'olau leaf axil sandhopper. Endemic. O'ahu. Scavenger of plant debris). One of several species of endemic arboreal sandhoppers, this species lives in leaf axils of* **'ie'ie** (**Freycinetia arborea**) *and* **pa'iniu** (**Astelia**). *This one is poised to hop.*

15▲

16▲ 17▼

19▲

MILLIPEDES

19. **Polyxenus hawaiiensis**? *(Polyxenidae. Hawaiian bristly millipede. Endemic? O'ahu. Under loose bark, in leaf litter in mesic forests. Scavenger).*

20. **Nannolene** *species (Undescribed. Cambalidae. Cave millipede. Endemic. Big Island. Fungus feeder. Lava tubes). It commonly has water drops hanging on it, since its subterranean environment is constantly saturated with water vapor.*

CENTIPEDES

21. **Lithobius** *species (Undescribed. Lithobiida(Cave rock centipede. Endemic. East Maui lava tubes. Predator and scavenger).*

DAMSELFLIES

22. **Megalagrion blackburni** *(Male. Coenagrionidae. Large red damselfly. Endemic. Moloka'i, Maui, Big Island. Breeds in streams and pools. Predator). Largest Hawaiian damselfly (more than 60 mm in body length).*

20▲ 21▼

23. **Megalagrion calliphya** *(Male. Coenagrionidae. Endemic. Maui, Moloka'i, Lāna'i. Breeds in pools. Predator).* This slender red damselfly species hawks insects in forest clearings, along upland streams, and in bogs. A parasitic water mite rides on the thorax of this specimen.

24. **Megalagrion nigrolineatum** *(Female. Coenagrionidae. Black-lined damselfly. Endemic. O'ahu. Breeds in streams. Predator).* The immature stages are aquatic and occur in stream pools. They have long, leaf-like tail gills typical of damselflies elsewhere. Once abundant in streams on O'ahu, this species has declined drastically since 1980 following the introduction of additional foreign fish species into O'ahu streams.

25. **Megalagrion peles** *(Female. Coenagrionidae. Endemic. Big Island. Breeds in leaf axils. Predator).* Adults of this diminutive species (30 mm, 1.25 inch, body length) hawk insects in the vicinity of their breeding sites in rain forests.

23▲   24▼   2

26. **Megalagrion koelense** *(Naiad or immature. Coenagrionidae. Endemic. O'ahu, Maui, Lāna'i, Big Island. Breeds in plant leaf axils. Predator). Naiads of this species breed in leaf axils of* **'ie'ie (Freycinetia arborea)** *and* **pa'iniu (Astelia menziesiana)**. *Like* **Megalagrion peles**, M. koelense *shows adaptations for damp rather than aquatic habitats.*

27. **Megalagrion hawaiiense** *(Male. Coenagrionidae. Hawaiian damselfly. Endemic. O'ahu, Maui Nui and Big Island. Breeds in streams, pools, and on wet rocks. Predator). Populations on O'ahu, Maui Nui and Big Island, probably represent different species. The adults of this and many* **Megalagrion** *species play possum when disturbed, a unique behavior within the order Odonata.*

28. **Megalagrion peles** *(Naiad). The immatures are common in leaf axils of* **Astelia** *in the* '**Ōla'a** *rain forest. The axils hold damp leaf mold and little water, and the naiad shows terrestrial adaptations, having short, thickened terminal gills, rather than the long, leaf-like swimming gills of aquatic damselflies.*

26▲   27▼   2

29. **Megalagrion oceanicum** (*Naiad. Coenagrionidae. Endemic. O'ahu. Breeds in streams. Predator*). *Adults are bright red and resemble* **M. blackburni** *found on the younger islands. Naiads crawl on the bottoms of stream pools and riffles.*

GRASSHOPPERS, KATYDIDS, CRICKETS

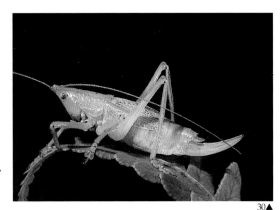
30.▲

30. **Banza nitida** (*Female. Tettigoniidae. Native cone-headed katydid. Endemic. Big Island. Mid-elevation rain forests. Omnivore*). *An endemic genus of short-winged, flightless, cone-headed grasshoppers.*

31. **Banza nitida**. *Males sing to call females, and each species has a distinct song composed of short bursts of high-pitched buzzes: "zzzt zzzt zzzt."*

32. **Banza unica** (*Male. Tettigoniidae. Native cone-headed katydid. Endemic. O'ahu. Mesic to wet forests. Omnivore*). *The 11 kinds discovered evolved from a single long-winged ancestral species.*

32▼   31▲

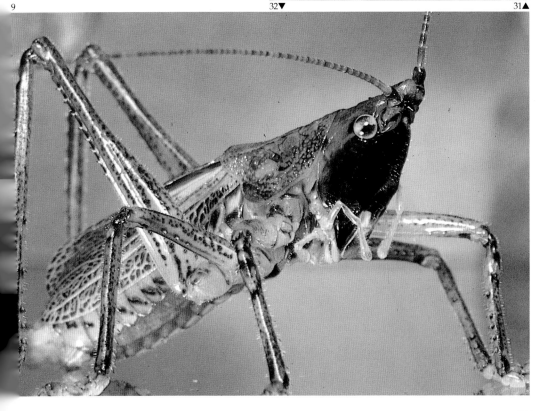

33▲

34▲

33. **Euconocephalus nasutus** *(Female. Tettigoniidae. Non-native cone-headed katydid. All islands from Nihoa to Big Island. Lowlands. Omnivore). After arrival, this pestiferous species quickly dispersed to the other islands. It resembles the presumed ancestor of* **Banza***.*

34. **Laupala** *(?) species (Nymphal male. Gryllidae. Native tinkling swordtail cricket. Endemic. Big Island. Lowlands to mid-elevation mesic and wet forests. Omnivore). Swordtail crickets are the most common and most diverse, with more than 150 species in two groups based on song: "trillers" and "tinklers."*

35. **Prognathogryllus alatus** *(Male. Gryllidae. Native tree cricket. Endemic. O'ahu. Mesic to wet forests. Omnivore). Males produce loud, musical trills by rubbing together their specialized front pair of wings. Females are mute.*

36. **Anaxipha atroferugineum** *(Female. Gryllidae. Native trilling swordtail cricket. Endemic. Moloka'i. Rain forests. Omnivore). Swordtail crickets sing both day and night from hidden perches and provide the voices for the fabled "singing" tree snails of Hawai'i.*

35▼   3●

37. **Partulina mighelsiana** (*Achatinellinae. A "singing" tree snail. Endemic. Moloka'i. Rain forests. Leaf surface gleaner*). *After early explorers brought these colorful shells back to Europe with the story that the animals could sing, the fable of the "singing" tree snails of Hawai'i both charmed and intrigued naturalists in Europe for more than 50 years before crickets were revealed as the source of the song.*

38. **Leptogryllus fusconotatus** (*Female. Gryllidae. Native tree cricket. Endemic. O'ahu. Mesic to wet forests. Omnivore*). *These crickets often hide by day in hollow stems.*

39. **Prognathogryllus** *species* (*Undescribed. Male. Gryllidae. Native tree cricket. Endemic. Big Island. Wet forest. Omnivore*). *This recently discovered species from the Kohala Mountains is undescribed. Since the songs are loud and distinctive, the ranges of each species can be precisely known, and some species are restricted to very small areas on a single island.*

37▲   38▼

40▲

41▲   42▼

40. Leptogryllus similis? *(Male. Gryllidae. Native tree cricket. Endemic. Big Island. Wet forests. Omnivore). Its front wings and those of the closely related* **Thaumatogryllus** *are reduced to tiny flaps and cannot produce sound. Their hind wings are absent.*

41. Thaumatogryllus *species (Undescribed. Female. Gryllidae. Maui cave tree cricket. Endemic. East Maui lava tubes. Omnivore). This species lives in a constantly dark, water vapor–saturated environment.*

42. Thaumatogryllus cavicola *(Female. Gryllidae. Big Island. Cave tree cricket. Endemic. Lava tubes. Omnivore). Some Hawaiian tree crickets have secondarily adapted to live on the ground, and different species live on dry talus slopes, rain forests, and caves. The cave species prefer to walk upside-down on the ceiling, feeding on roots that dangle into the cave.*

43. Caconemobius *species A (Undescribed. Female. Gryllidae. Hawaiian splash zone cricket. Endemic. Nihoa to Big Island. Boulder beaches. Scavenger). This marine cricket lives in the wet-rock zone on wave-splashed boulder beaches in the islands.*

44▲

45▲

44. **Caconemobius** species A (Undescribed. Male). Close-up of the Hawaiian beach cricket, showing dark color, big eyes, and lack of wings.

45. **Caconemobius fori** (Male. Gryllidae. Lava flow cricket. Endemic. Big Island. Young, unvegetated lava flows. Omnivore). Close-up, showing large eyes and dark color. This species appears to have evolved from the splash zone cricket. These crickets hide in cracks in the lava during the day and come to the surface at night to search for food.

46. **Caconemobius** species B (Undescribed. Female. Gryllidae. Maui lava tube cricket. Endemic. East Maui. Omnivore). This species evolved from a splash zone ancestor independently of the Big Island cave species, yet has undergone similar adaptive changes.

47. **Caconemobius varius** (Female. Gryllidae. Big Island cave cricket. Endemic. Lava tubes. Omnivore). Close-up showing the reduced eyes and pale color characteristic of cave adaptation. This species appears to have evolved from the lava flow cricket.

46▼

48▲

EARWIGS

48. **Anisolabis howarthi** *(Male. Carcinophoridae. Hawaiian cave earwig. Endemic. Big Island lava tubes. Predator). Prefers living in cracks and crannies of lava.*

TRUE BUGS

49. **Mesovelia amoena** *(Female. Mesoveliidae. Water treader. Foreign. Kaua'i to Big Island. Semi-aquatic. Predator/scavenger). Generally live by shores and on surface of quiet pools.*

50. **Speovelia aaa** *(Male. Mesoveliidae. Lava tube water treader. Endemic. Big Island lava tubes. Scavenger). Wanders in damp caves feeding on rotting juices of long-dead arthropods.*

51. **Saldula oahuensis**? *(Saldidae. Shore bugs. Endemic. Kaua'i to Big Island. Moist habitats. Predator.) An arboreal species.*

52. **Cyrtopeltis confusa** *(Miridae. Mirid leaf bug. Endemic. O'ahu. Mesic to wet forests, on* **Cyrtandra**. *Sap sucker). One of three species of* **Cyrtopeltis** *endemic to O'ahu.*

50▲   51▼   52▼

53▲

54▲   55▼

53. **Nesiomiris** *species (Undescribed. Female. Miridae. Mirid leaf bug. Endemic. Big Island wet forests. On* **Cheirodendron trigynum***). This genus has extensively radiated, with more than 50 species in the islands. Most are found on only one island, and each attacks a narrow range of hosts within the Araliaceae and Aquifoliaceae.*

54. **Nesidiorchestes** *species near* **hawaiiensis** *(Undescribed. Miridae. Mirid leaf bug. Endemic. West Maui wet forests. Leaf litter. Predaceous?). This genus was previously known from a single species on O'ahu, until this similar species was found on West Maui. A strong jumper.*

55. **Kalania** *species (Undescribed. Female. Miridae. Mirid leaf bug. Endemic. West Maui. On* **Urera glabra***. Sap sucker). Only a few specimens of this exceedingly rare endemic genus are known. The genus is so unusual that it is placed in its own tribe.*

56. **Pseudoclerada kilaueae** *(Female. Miridae. Mirid leaf bug. Endemic. Big Island wet forests. Possibly predaceous). The genus is known from Kaua'i to the Big Island, and each island probably has one or more endemic species.*

57. **Nesidiorchestes** *species (Undescribed. Miridae. Mirid leaf bug. Endemic. Big Island wet forest. Possibly predaceous). The third species of* **Nesidiorchestes** *is a creeper, not a jumper. Compare with figure 54.*

58. **Nesidiolestes** *species (Undescribed. Nymph. Reduviidae. Emesinae. Thread-legged bug. Endemic. West Maui. Rain forests. Predator). The thread-legged bugs capture arthropods with their praying mantis–like front legs and hold their prey off the surface with their long stilt legs.*

59. **Saicella** *species (Nymph and its egg case. Undescribed. Emesinae. Endemic. Big Island. Predator). The eggs hatch in about 35 days.*

60. **Nesidiolestes ana** *(Mating pair. Reduviidae. Emesinae. Big Island cave thread-legged bug. Endemic. Lava tubes. Predator). With its slender build, long legs and antennae, this bug looks admirably adapted to caves.*

61. **Nabis tarai** *(Nymph. Nabidae. Damsel bug. Endemic. Kaua'i to the Big Island. Predator). This nymph molted to the adult shown in figure 62.*

57▲   58▼   60▼   6

59▼

62▲

63▲

62. **Nabis** *species near* **N. lolupe** *(Undescribed. Female. Nabidae. Damsel bug. Endemic. Kaua'i. Rain forests. Predator). The tiny wings and delicate green color of this damsel bug belie its predatory habits.*

63. **Nabis oscillans** *(Female. Endemic. Big Island. Rain forests. Predator). This dark, cryptically colored damsel bug hunts for prey in the deep shadows of mossy rain forests.*

64. **Nabis curtipennis** *(Female. Endemic. Big Island. Rain forests. Predator). This lateral view reveals the sucking beak, or rostrum, characteristic of the true bugs (Heteroptera).*

65. **Nabis tarai** *(Endemic. Damsel bug. Endemic. Many habitats. Kaua'i to Big Island. Predator). A newly emerged adult is shown with its cast nymphal skin. Figure 61 shows the same animal just before molting.*

64▼   6

66. **Ithamar hawaiiensis** *(Rhopalidae. Scentless plant bugs. Endemic. O'ahu, Maui Nui, and Big Island. Host:* **pūkiawe***).* **Ithamar** *is an unusual endemic genus, with apparently no close relative outside of Hawai'i.*

67. *Rhyparochrominae (Undescribed genus and species. Lygaeidae. Endemic. O'ahu. Rain forests. Seed feeder in leaf litter). This strange beetle-like bug was discovered in 1973 on O'ahu. Subsequent search turned up additional species on Kaua'i and the Big Island. These represent a hitherto overlooked native group in Hawai'i. What other surprises await discovery in the Hawaiian natural environment?*

68. **Coleotichus blackburniae** *(Scutelleridae.* **Koa** *bug. Endemic. All islands from Kaua'i to the Big Island. Hosts:* **koa** *and* **'a'ali'i***). The largest and most conspicuous native true bug has a variable color pattern, often with beautiful iridescent hues. See page 30.*

66▲   67▼   6

69▲

70▲   71▼

69. **Nysius wekiuicola** *(Lygaeidae. Wekiu bug. Endemic. Big Island. Summits of Mauna Kea and Mauna Loa. Scavenger).*

LEAFHOPPERS, PLANT–HOPPERS, SCALE INSECTS

70. **Nesophrosyne** *species (Undescribed. Cicadellidae. Leafhopper. Endemic. Big Island. Rain forests. Host:* **Clermontia***).*

71. **Nesophrosyne** *species (Nymph. Cicadellidae. Leafhopper. Endemic. Big Island. Rain forests. Host:* **Myrsine***). Often live on the undersides of leaves.*

72. **Oliarus** *species A (Undescribed. Cixiidae. Cixiid planthopper. Endemic. West Maui. Rain forests. Nymphs feed on plant roots). Most have long wings, big eyes, hopping hind legs, and somber body colors.*

73. **Oliarus polyphemus** *(Female. Cixiidae. Big Island cave cixiid planthopper. Endemic. Lava tubes. Roots of* **'ōhi'a lehua***). Short wings, no eyes, small jumping legs, and no body color.*

73▼

97

74▲

74. **Oliarus** *species B (Undescribed. Female. Cixiidae. Maui cave cixiid planthopper. Endemic. East Maui. Lava tubes. Roots of* **'ōhi'a lehua***). In an example of parallel evolution, the two pictured cave planthoppers evolved independently from separate surface ancestors.*

75. **Nesosydne** *species (Undescribed? Delphacidae. Delphacid planthopper. Endemic. West Maui. Rain forests. Host:* **Cyanea***). Probably the adult form of the nymph in figure 76.*

76. **Nesosydne** *(?) species (Undescribed? Nymph. Delphacidae. Delphacid planthopper. Endemic. West Maui. Rain forests. Host:* **Cyanea***). The sac-like larva attached to the side of this nymph is probably a dryinid wasp, introduced to control foreign pestiferous planthoppers in lowland agricultural fields.*

77. **Dictyophorodelphax mirabilis** *(Delphacidae. Delphacid planthopper. Endemic. O'ahu. Dry to mesic forests. Host:* **Euphorbia***). The elongate head may be an adaptation to handle the toxic sap of their native* **Euphorbia** *host plants.*

75▲   76▼

78. **Dictyophorodelphax swezeyi** *(Male and female. Delphacidae. Delphacid planthopper. Endemic. O'ahu. Dry to mesic forests. Host:* **Euphorbia***). The elongate heads make these insects look like thorns on* **Euphorbia** *stems. A branch of the gut extends to the tip of the horn and may help digest the toxic sap or simply store the toxin to discourage predators.*

79. *Pseudococcidae (Unidentified. Pseudococcidae. Mealybug. Foreign? Big Island. Lava tube. Host: plant roots). There are about 30 described species of endemic Hawaiian mealybugs placed in 12 genera.*

LACEWINGS, ANTLIONS

80. **Nesomicromus vagus** *(Hemerobiidae. Brown lacewing. Endemic. All islands from Kaua'i to the Big Island. Many habitats). Brown lacewings are avid predators of aphids, psocids, and other small arthropods. The adult body form of most is similar to this species, but some marvels of island evolution have occurred in this group in Hawai'i.*

78▲   79▼

81▲

82▲

83▼

81. **Pseudopsectra lobipennis** *(Hemerobiidae. Flightless brown lacewing. Endemic. Haleakalā, East Maui. Rain forests. Predator). This species no longer has lace wings but has hardened beetle-like front wings and vestigial hind wings. The adults hunt at night on tree trunks in rain forests.*

82. **Nesomicromus paradoxus** *(Hemerobiidae. Brown lacewing. Endemic. Moloka'i and Big Island. Rain forests. Extremely rare). The function of the unusual wing shape is unknown. The two island populations appear to be distinct. This specimen is from Moloka'i.*

83. **Pseudopsectra swezeyi** *(Hemerobiidae. Swezey's flightless brown lacewing. Endemic. Kaua'i. Wet rain forest floor. Extremely rare). This flightless predator plays dead when disturbed.* **Pseudopsectra lobipennis** *and this species appear to have evolved independently from different ancestors within* **Nesomicromus***.*

84. **Anomalochrysa** *species (Unidentified. Chrysopidae. Hawaiian green lacewing). This is a common species on the Big Island.*

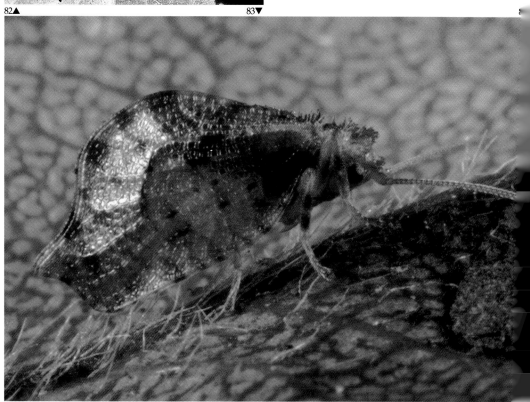

85. **Eidoleon** *species (Undescribed. Myrmeleontidae. Kaua'i antlion. Endemic. Mesic forest. Predator. Rare). Native antlions survive on at least Kaua'i, Kaho'olawe, and the Big Island. The larvae are poorly known, but, contrary to many continental species, they do not build pits, nor do they prey on ants.*

86. **Anomalochrysa** *species (Unidentified. Chrysopidae). This glassy-winged species was collected on Moloka'i.*

87. **Anomalochrysa** *species. This color form was collected on Moloka'i but is also known from the Big Island.*

85▲   86▼   87

BEETLES

88. **Dromaeolus arduus** (*Eucnemidae. False click beetle. Endemic. O'ahu and Big Island. Mesic and wet forests. Probably a woodborer*).

89. **Parandra puncticeps** (*Cerambycidae. Long-horned woodborer. Endemic. All islands. Larvae in dead wood*). *This large woodborer (up to 25 mm, 1 inch) tunnels in the dead wood of many tree species.*

90. **Megopis reflexa** (*Cerambycidae. Long-horned woodborer. Endemic. All islands. Larvae in dead wood*). *This species is the largest native beetle (up to 50 mm, 2 inches). The large larva tunnels in dead wood.*

91. Plagithmysus montgomeryi
(Cerambycidae. Long-horned woodborer.
Endemic. Mauna Kea, Big Island. Montane dry
forest. Host: **Chamaesyce olowaluana**). A rare
species on a rare host.

92. Plagithmysus urerae (Cerambycidae.
Long-horned woodborer. Endemic. West Maui.
Wet forests. Host: **Urera glabra**).

93. Plagithmysus varians (Endemic. Big
Island. Mesic to wet forests. Host: **Acacia koa**).

91▲   92▼   9

94. **Proterhinus** *species (Aglycyderidae. Endemic. O'ahu. Mesic forests). About 170 species are known in this genus, but estimates of endemic species range up to 250. The larval habitat of each species is very narrow, but the species, in concert, feed on nearly all native woody plant species as well as on larger ferns. They are twig-, stem-, and woodborers; a few are even leaf miners.*

95. **Oodemus** *species (Curculionidae. Endemic. Laysan, Kaua'i to Big Island. Woodborers).* **Oodemus** *weevils are dark and shiny with a metallic sheen and resemble seeds. Their larvae are mostly twig- and woodborers on a wide range of plants.*

96. **Anotheorus** *species (Curculionidae. Endemic. O'ahu. Mesic to wet forests. Wood borers).* **Anotheorus** *and the related* **Oodemus** *are flightless weevils and have no known close relatives outside of Hawai'i and may be an ancient relict group, for example, one that island-hopped down the chain.*

94▲   95▼   9

97▲

98▲

97. **Stenotrupis prolixum** *(Curculionidae.* **Hāpu'u** *weevil. Endemic. Big Island. Rain forests.* **Cibotium** *fern fronds). The elongate shape of the weevil is admirably suited to negotiate the narrow, pulpy channels running the length of rotting* **hāpu'u** *(tree fern) stems.*

98. **Nesotocus monroi***? (Female. Curculionidae. Endemic. Big Island. Rain forests. Host: Araliaceae trees). These weevils remain an enigma. They have diverged so far from their relatives that even the placement of* **Nesotocus** *in the proper subfamily is uncertain.*

99. **Nesotocus monroi***? (Male.) The long, spindly legs and position of the antennae on the snout mark this individual as a male.*

100. **Rhynchogonus molokaiensis** *(Curculionidae. Endemic. Moloka'i. Rain forests). This rarely collected species is the only known member of the genus on Moloka'i. All species in this genus of large weevils are flightless.*

100▼   9

101. Rhynchogonus giffardi? *(Female. Curculionidae. Endemic. Dry shrublands. Host:* **Dodonaea**). *This is the only species on the Big Island and is one of the rarest Hawaiian weevils, with a severely restricted known range of no more than one acre.*

102. Rhynchogonus welchi *(Female. Endemic. O'ahu. Mesic forest. Host:* **Sapindus**). *The largest (20 mm, 0.8 inch) and most boldly marked native weevil, it lives only in a small area of the Wai'anae Mountains on O'ahu.*

103. Rhynchogonus tubercullatus *(Female. Endemic. Wet forests. Host:* **Hedyotis**). *One of about 20 species endemic to Kaua'i, this one was collected on* **Hedyotis**.

104. Rhynchogonus koebelei *(Female. Endemic. O'ahu. Wet forest). One of about a dozen species endemic to O'ahu, it has a restricted range in the Ko'olau Mountains. The adults feed on* **Broussaisia**, **Hedyotis**, *and* **Pelea**.

101▲   102▼

103▼   1

105. **Rhynchogonus stygius** *(Male. Curculionidae. Endemic. Kaua'i. Mesic forests. Host:* **koa***).* **Rhynchogonus** *larvae live in the soil and probably feed on roots.*

106. **Rhynchogonus** *species A (Female. Undescribed. Endemic. Kaua'i. Mesic forests. Host:* **Hedyotis**, **Pelea***). Even though this genus was considered relatively well known, new species like this one continue to be discovered.*

107. **Rhynchogonus** *species B (Female. Undescribed. Endemic. Kaua'i. Wet forest.* **Scaevola**, **Perrottetia**, *etc). This species resembles* **Rhynchogonus tubercullatus**, *but the tubercles are even more prominent.*

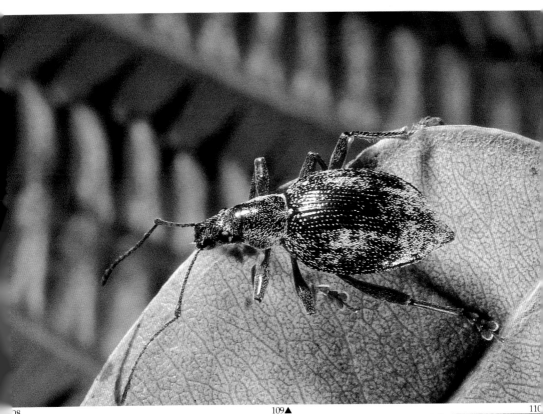

08

109▲

110

108. **Rhynchogonus** *species C (Male. Curculionidae. Undescribed. Endemic. Kaua'i. Mesic forest.* **Pisonia**, **Psychotria**, *etc). The snowshoe-like feet allow these weevils to walk on smooth leaf surfaces.*

109. **Rhynchogonus** *species D (Female. Undescribed. Endemic. Kaua'i. Mesic forest. Host:* **'ōhi'a lehua***).*

MOTHS, BUTTERFLIES

110. **Spheterista** *species (Undescribed. Tortricidae. Leaf rollers. Endemic. 18 known species. Kaua'i to Big Island). The known species are leaf-tiers and twig, bud, and fruit borers.*

111. **Plutella** *species (Undescribed. Plutellidae. Diamondback moths. Endemic. Kaua'i to Big Island? Coastal and dry forest). Feeds on native* **Capparis***, an uncommon plant of the lowlands. Each island may harbor one or more endemic species.*

11

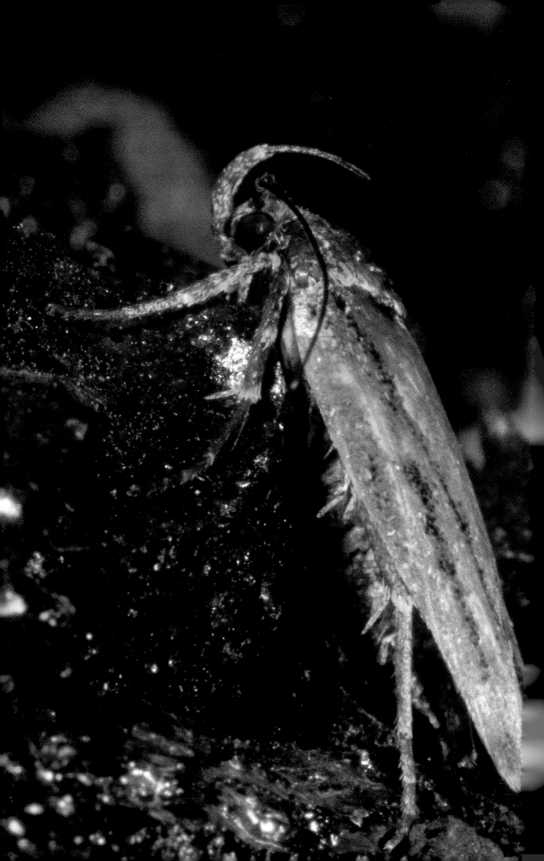

112. Thyrocopa apatela *(Female. Oecophoridae. Endemic. East Maui. Alpine and aeolian zones. Scavenger). Adults of both sexes are short winged and flightless. They flutter in the wind resembling dried leaves, and are blown to appropriate deposits of debris in which to mate and lay eggs.*

113. Thyrocopa apatela *(Larva. Endemic. East Maui. Alpine and aeolian zones. Scavenger). Larvae make web nests, eat dried leaves and other organic debris deposited in cracks and under large rocks and scattered bushes near the summit of Haleakalā.*

114. Hyposmocoma oculifera *(Cosmopterigidae. Endemic. Kaua'i. Mesic to wet forests. Unknown biology). The 350 known species in the genus* **Hyposmocoma** *represent one of the most spectacular examples of adaptive radiation anywhere.*

115. Hyposmocoma sagittata *(Cosmopterigidae. Endemic. Kaua'i. Mesic to wet forests. Unknown biology).*

113▲

112

115▼

114▲

121

116▲

116. **Carposina** *species (Undescribed.*
Carposinidae. **Loulu** *fruit moth. Endemic. Big*
Island. Rain forests). Carposinid larvae bore in
fruits. This undescribed species feeds in the fruits
of the native Hawaiian palm, **loulu**.

117. **Udea swezeyi** *(Crambidae. Endemic.*
Kaua'i. Mesic to wet forests. Unknown biology).

118. **Udea eucrena** *(Crambidae. Endemic.*
Kaua'i, O'ahu, Maui, Big Island. Host:
Phyllostegia*). This boldly marked species often*
rests with its abdomen upturned. The larvae feed
on native mints. This specimen is from Kaua'i.

119. **Udea** *species near* **U. pyranthes**
(Undescribed. Crambidae. Endemic. Big Island.
Wet forests. Host: **Vaccinium***).* **U. pyranthes**
lives on Kaua'i and look-alike species live on the
younger islands.

117▲   118▼   11⁹

120. **Hyles calida** (*Sphingidae. Endemic. Kaua'i, O'ahu, Maui, Moloka'i. Many hosts*). *These hawk moths have a wingspan of about 65 mm (2.5 inches). The larvae have been found on many hosts but prefer the native members of the coffee family, especially* **Coprosma**, **Psychotria**, *and* **Hedyotis**.

121. **Manduca blackburni** (*Larva. Sphingidae. Blackburn hawk moth. Endemic. Kaua'i to Big Island. Coastal and dry forests. Host: Solanaceae*). *This species is now known only from Maui.*

122. **Manduca blackburni** (*Adult*). *This species is a close relative of the tomato hornworm of North America.*

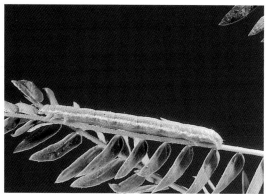

123▲

124▲

123. **Semiothesa abydata** *(Larva. Geometridae.* **Koa haole** *moth. Foreign. Widespread. Lowlands). This recent immigrant species is sometimes abundant when defoliating the alien weedy shrub* **koa haole (Leucaena leucocephala).** *This larva displays the twig-mimicking behavior and general body form of the inchworms (Geometridae).*

124. **Fletcherana** *species (Geometridae. Endemic. Wet forests. Unknown biology).* **Fletcherana** *has five described species. This beautiful moth from Kaua'i is an undescribed representative of the group.*

125. **Eupithecia monticolens** *(Female. Geometridae. Endemic. Kaua'i to Big Island. Dry to wet forests. Host:* **'ōhi'a lehua).** **Eupithecia** *provides one of the most spectacular stories in Hawaiian natural history. The biology of this species may be close to that of the original colonizer for this group.*

126. **Eupithecia monticolens** *(Larva). A typical inchworm larva, which, like many* **Eupithecia** *species elsewhere, has adapted to feeding on flowers and pollen.*

125▼

1.

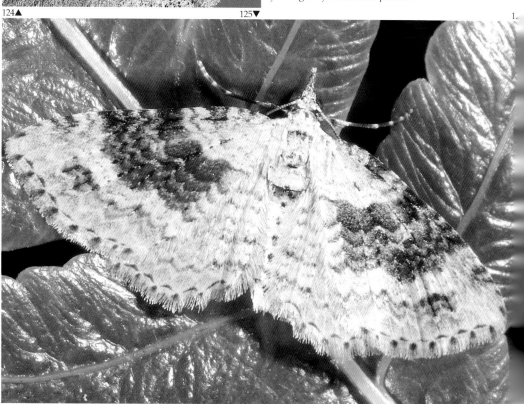

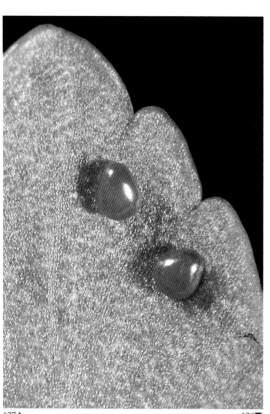

127. **Eupithecia orichloris** (*Eggs. Geometridae. Endemic. Kaua'i to Big Island. Mesic to wet forests. Predator*). *The female moth lays only one or a few eggs at a time on the undersides of leaves. These two eggs are on a sword fern frond* (**Nephrolepis**).

128. **Eupithecia orichloris**. *Hatchling larva (2 mm, 0.1 inch) with egg shell and unhatched sibling. The posture and form of the young larva suggest its predatory nature.*

129. **Eupithecia orichloris**. *Hatchling larva devouring its first meal, a bark louse (Psocoptera). This and the following species are the world's first known ambushing predatory caterpillars.*

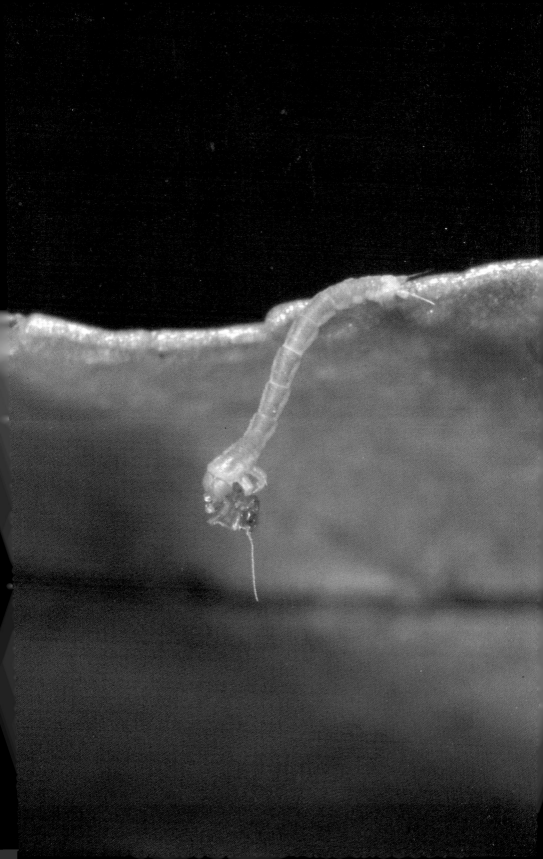

130. **Eupithecia orichloris**. *Full-grown larva (25 mm, 1 inch) waits in characteristic pose along a leaf edge. A native fly (***Drosophila conspicua***) explores the leaf dangerously close to the specialized sensory hairs on the hind end of the caterpillar, which trigger the predator's strike.*

131. **Eupithecia orichloris**. *Gotcha! A full-grown caterpillar has just captured a fly (***Drosophila conspicua***) with its strong legs and long, sharp claws, and feeds on its struggling prey.*

132. **Eupithecia orichloris**. *Adult female from the Big Island with an unusual gold color. Green is the usual color of these attractive moths. See page 15.*

130▲   131▼   1

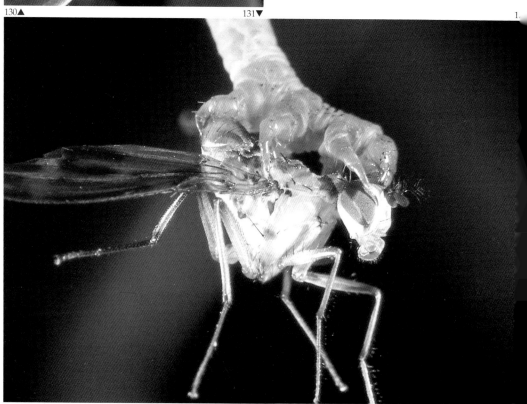

133▲

134▲

135▼

133. **Eupithecia staurophragma** (*Adult female. Geometridae. Endemic. O'ahu, Moloka'i, Maui, Big Island. Dry to wet forests. Twig-mimicking ambush predator*). This moth with a 25-mm wingspan rests on tree fern foliage.

134. **Eupithecia craterias** (*Male. Geometridae. Endemic. Moloka'i. Maui, Big Island. Mesic to wet forests. Ambush predator*). As with the larvae, the adults come in many color patterns. Its wingspan is 20 mm (0.8 inches).

135. **Eupithecia staurophragma** (*Larva*). The larvae favor twigs as hunting perches. This Big Island caterpillar gorges on a large captured fly (**Drosophila heteroneura**).

136. **Eupithecia scoriodes** (*Larva. Geometridae. Endemic. East Maui. Alpine scrub zone. Ambush predator*). A twig-like caterpillar in hunting posture waits for an insect or spider walking by on the stem to touch its hind end, whereupon it will lash back and capture its prey.

137. **Eupithecia** *species near* **rhodopyra** (*Undescribed. Geometridae. Endemic. O'ahu, Molokai, Maui. Rain forests. Ambush predator*). An adult male from O'ahu of this distinctive species rests on a fern frond.

136▼   1

138▲

138. **Eupithecia scoriodes** (*Geometridae. Endemic. East Maui. Alpine scrub. Ambush predator*). *Adults are normally darker than this. Unlike other Hawaiian* **Eupithecia**, *adults fly during the day and behave like butterflies on the upper slopes of Haleakalā. The cold nights at this altitude limit nocturnal activity of insects.*

139. **Eupithecia** *species A (Undescribed. Geometridae. Endemic. Moloka'i, Maui. Montane rain forests. Ambush predator). Resembling liverworts with their unusual shape, tubercles, spines, and color, this larva is well camouflaged, waiting for prey among the mosses and liverworts on tree branches in cloud forests.*

140. **Eupithecia** *species A. The adult moth rests on the mossy habitat of its larval stage.*

141. **Haliophyle** *species near* **flavistigma** (*Undescribed. Noctuidae. Endemic. Moloka'i. Rain forests. Host: ferns?). This moth belongs to an apparently undescribed species related to* **Haliophyle flavistigma** *known from Maui.*

142. **Haliophyle euclidias?** (*Noctuidae. Endemic. Kaua'i. Rain forests. Host: ferns). The larvae feed on ferns, but the biologies of most other species are unknown.*

139▲   140▼

142▼

143▲

143. **Lophoplusia** *species near* **pterylota** *(Larva. Noctuidae. Endemic. West Maui. Rain forests. Host: native lobelias). This larva was found on* **Cyanea** *and reared on* **Clermontia** *leaves.*

144. **Lophoplusia** *species near* **pterylota** *(Adult). The adult of the larva shown in figure 143 has a wingspan of nearly 40 mm (1.5 inches).* **Lophoplusia** *is an endemic genus with four described species, but more species are represented in collections.*

145. **Lophoplusia** *species near* **violacea** *(Larva. Noctuidae. Endemic. Big Island. Rain forests. Host: native lobelias). This larva was found and reared on* **Clermontia** *near Volcano on Kilauea. The larvae hide in leaf litter during the day and climb the host plant to feed at night.*

146. **Lophoplusia** *species near* **violacea** *(Adult). The reared adult of the same species as figure 145, showing the complex color pattern. This group is only occasionally attracted to lights.*

145▲

146▼

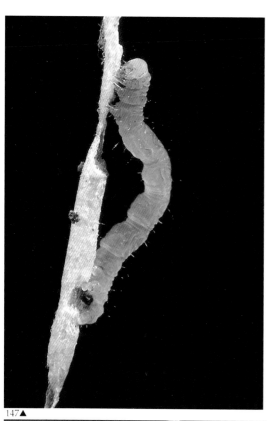

147. **Schrankia** species (Larva. Undescribed. Noctuidae. Big Island cave moth. Endemic. Lava tubes. Host: roots). The cave moth larvae feed on succulent tips of plant roots deep in caves. They may also scavenge on organic debris. Several species live in caves amd show different levels of cave adaptation.

148. **Schrankia** species (Undescribed). Female on its cocoon. **Schrankia** larvae build their cocoons out of root fragments attached to a hanging root. The adult female is flightless and, as shown here, sits on the cocoon in the dark "calling" males by emitting a pheromone from the tip of her abdomen.

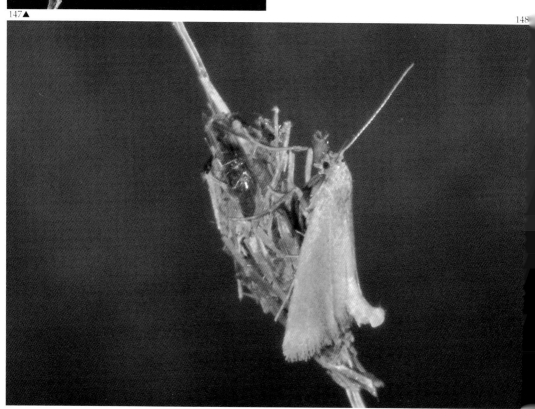

149. Udara blackburni *(Female. Lycaenidae. Blackburn butterfly. Endemic. Kaua'i to Big Island. Coastal to alpine shrub. Host: **Koa**, **'a'ali'i**, etc.). The delicate green underside of the wings distinguishes this species from introduced lycaenid butterflies. A fast and erratic flier, its wingspan is about 18 mm (0.75 inches).*

150. Udara blackburni *(Female). One of only two native butterflies, the Blackburn is widespread in the islands. Its caterpillars feed on flowers and buds, especially native legumes and soapberries. The caterpillar is well camouflaged on the flowers of its preferred host, **koa**. This female sits on **'a'ali'i**, another favorite host.*

149▲

151. **Vanessa tameamea** (Chrysalis. Nymphalidae. Kamehameha butterfly. Endemic. Kaua'i to Big Island. Host: native nettles). The chrysalis resembles a curled dead leaf of **māmaki** and is often hard to detect on the host plant. The adult emerges in just over two weeks.

152. **Vanessa tameamea** (Larva). Kamehameha butterfly caterpillars feed on the native nettles and are most commonly found on **māmaki** (**Pipturus**). Young caterpillars are leafrollers; they form a shelter by cutting a crescent-shape flap, bending it over, and fastening the edge to the leaf surface with silk. Older caterpillars do not make shelters but feed on exposed leaves.

151▲

152▼

153. **Vanessa tameamea** (*Female*). *Whereas the pattern on the upper wing surface varies little, the pattern on the undersurface is highly variable. Adults are strong fliers and most active on sunny days. They are attracted to sap oozing from tree wounds, especially on* **koa**.

154. **Vanessa tameamea** (*Female*). *Females have a wingspan of about 65 mm (2.5 inches). They are distinguishable from males by the upper wing surface having larger dark spots within the red patches along the hind margin of the hind wings, and by having a pair of white, rather than orange, spots on the front margin of the fore wing. See page 58.*

153▲

FLIES

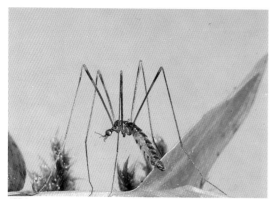

155▲

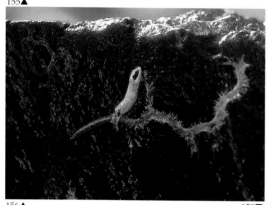

156▲

155. **Limonia hardyana** (*Female. Tipulidae. O'ahu flightless crane fly. Endemic. Wet rain forests*). This fly lives in the leaf litter and on mosses of tree trunks in the Ko'olau Mountains.

156. **Telmatogeton torrenticola** (*Larva. Chironomidae. Endemic. Maui. Fast-flowing streams. Scavenger*). A **Telmatogeton** *larva* emerges from its slime tunnel to feed on algae on a rock in a stream riffle.

157. **Aedes albopictus** (*Engorging female. Culicidae. Forest day mosquito. Foreign. Kaua'i to Big Island. Coastal and lowland forests*). This mosquito was inadvertently introduced in the late 1800s and continues to be an irritating pest in the lowlands.

158 Hawaiian long-legged fly (*Dolichopodidae. Endemic. All islands. Aquatic and damp habitats. Predators*). This is a large group with 200 described native species in seven genera.

158▼

15

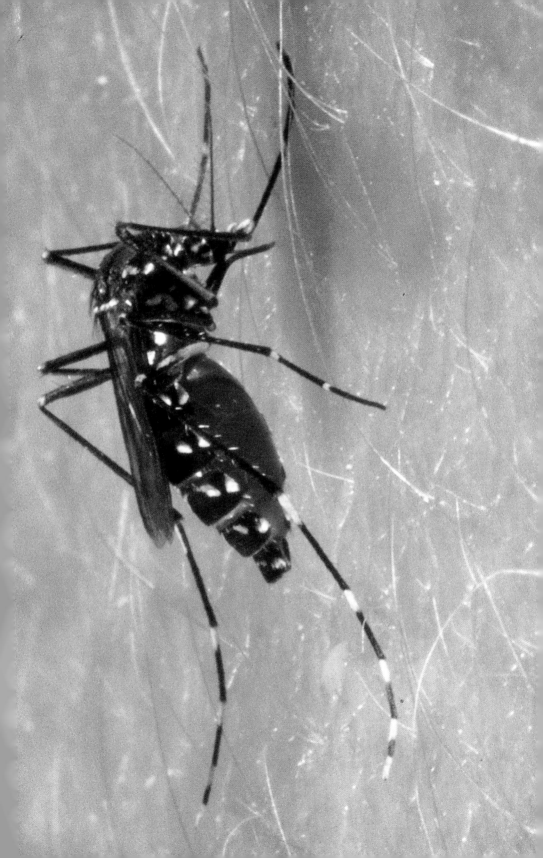

159. Campsicnemus haleakalaae
(Dolichopodidae. Endemic. East Maui. Rain forests. Leaf litter. Predator). This remarkable flightless fly, with vestigial wings, hops about like a large flea.

160. Trupanea denotata *(Tephritidae. Greensword fruit fly. Endemic. East Maui. Rain forest bog. Host: greensword). Larvae of this species feed on flower heads of greenswords high on Haleakalā.*

161. Trupanea *species A near* **T. cratericola**. *(Male. Tephritidae. Endemic. Big Island. Alpine shrub. Host: Silversword flowers?)*

162. Trupanea *species A near* **T. cratericola**. *The female has a long, black ovipositor.*

163. Phaeogramma hispida *(Male. Tephritidae. Endemic. West Maui. Dry forests. Host:* **Bidens** *stem gall). This is an endemic genus of stem gall breeders. Two species are described, and at least two more remain to be described.*

164▲

165▲   166▼

164. **Drosophila primaeva** (Drosophilidae. Endemic. Kaua'i. Wet forests. Host: native Araliaceae). This species has primitive features and is thought to be close to the ancestor of the "picture wings," a native group of over 100 species that have been the subject of intensive research for over 25 years.

165. **Drosophila cyrtoloma** (Hawaiian picture wing. Endemic. East Maui. Rain forests. Host: native Araliaceae). This may be the largest drosophilid in the world with a wingspan of over 20 mm (0.8 inches).

166. **Drosophila crucigera** (Male. Hawaiian picture wing. Endemic. Kaua'i, O'ahu. Mesic forests. Host: generalist). This close-up shows one of the many complex color patterns in the group.

167. **Drosophila heteroneura** (Males. Hawaiian picture wing. Endemic. Big island. Rain forests. Native lobelia bark). Here, two males bang heads and wave wings to gain superiority at a feeding site. These contests are very important in determining male dominance and mating success, through control of a lek or mating territory.

168. **Drosophila silvestris** *(Male and female. Hawaiian picture wing. Endemic. Big Island. Rain forests. Host: native lobelia bark). A male (below) displays his wings to a female (above) as part of his courtship ritual. Males of this species have a narrow head and dark face. This species and* **D. heteroneura** *produce fertile hybrids when crossed.*

169. **Drosophila grimshawi** *(Male. Hawaiian picture wing. Endemic. Kaua'i, O'ahu, Moloka'i, Lāna'i, and Maui. Host: generalist). Different island populations have different host preferences; flies from Kaua'i and O'ahu are restricted to* **Wikstroemia** *bark, while those from Maui Nui breed in a wide variety of hosts.*

170. **Drosophila pullipes** *(Male. Hawaiian picture wing. Endemic. Big Island. Wet forests. Host:* **Wikstroemia** *bark). This species evolved from a* **D. grimshawi** *that colonized the Big Island from one of the older islands. The only external differences between the two species are that* **D. pullipes** *has slightly darker legs and a few subtly darker areas on the thorax, but laboratory hybrids between the two species are sterile.*

168▲   169▼   17

171▲

172▲   173▼

171. **Titanochaeta bryani** (*Female with egg. Drosophilidae. Endemic. O'ahu, Maui Nui, Big Island. Mesic to wet forests. Prey on spider eggs).* **Titanochaeta** (*with 13 known species) is an odd endemic genus related to* **Scaptomyza.**

172. **Lispocephala** *species (Unidentified. Muscidae. Endemic. Maui. Wet forests. Predator). Recognizable by perky stance and quick, jerky movements while hunting.*

173. **Scaptomyza deludens** (*Diptera. Drosophilidae. Endemic. Big Island. Mesic forests. Host: morning glory flowers). Frequently seen in breeding site, like this* **Ipomoea** *flower.*

174. **Celidosoma nigrocincta** (*Male. Drosophilidae. Endemic. O'ahu, Lāna'i, Moloka'i. Mesic to wet forests. Unknown biology). In terms of external characteristics, this genus with its single species seems far removed from other Hawaiian drosophilids, but it is considered to have evolved from a native* **Scaptomyza** *species. Its biology remains unknown, and it is thought to have made a strange adaptive shift, like its relative* **Titanochaeta***.*

175▼

BEES, WASPS, ANTS

175. (Previous page). Ichneumonidae (Unidentified. Ichneumon wasp. Foreign? Big Island, possibly other islands. Caterpillar parasite). This parasite was reared from a predaceous caterpillar, **Eupithecia craterias**.

176. **Hylaeus** species (Unidentified. Colletidae. Endemic. Big Island. Dry forests. Nectar and pollen). Over 60 species of native yellow-faced bees are known. They live in most habitats from the coast to the alpine zone and are important pollinators of native plants.

177. **Platymischoides** species (Unidentified. Diapriidae. Endemic. East Maui. Rain forests. Parasite). This flightless ant-like wasp parasitizes fly larvae.

176▲   177▼

152

BIBLIOGRAPHY

GENERAL REFERENCES ON HAWAIIAN NATURAL HISTORY

ARMSTRONG, R.W., ed. *Atlas of Hawaii.* 2nd ed. Honolulu: Univ. of Hawaii Press, 1983.

CARLQUIST, S. *Hawaii, a Natural History. Geology, Climate, Native Flora and Fauna above the Shoreline.* 2nd ed. Pacific Tropical Botanic Garden, Lawai, Hawai'i, 1980.

DAWS, G. *Hawaii: The Islands of Life.* The Nature Conservancy of Hawai'i, Honolulu: Signature Publ., 1988.

DECKER, R.W., T.L. WRIGHT, and P.H. STAUFFER, eds. *Volcanism in Hawai'i.* U.S. Geol. Surv. Prof. Pap. 1350, 1987.

GRESSITT, J.L., ed. *Pacific Basin Biogeography.* Honolulu: Bishop Museum Press, 1963.

KAY, E.A., ed. *A Natural History of the Hawaiian Islands—Selected Readings.* Honolulu: Univ. of Hawaii Press, 1976.

MILLER, J.M., ed. "Hawaii's Unique Biology." *BioScience* 38 (1988): 232–282.

MUELLER-DOMBOIS, D., K.W. BRIDGES, and H.L. CARSON, eds. *Island Ecosystems: Biological Organization in Selected Hawaiian Communities.* Vol. 15. US/IBP Synthesis Series. Stroudsburg, Penn.: Hutchinson Ross Pub. Co., 1981.

SIMON, C.M., and A. SUGDEN, eds. "Hawaiian Evolutionary Biology." *Trends Ecol. Evol.* 2 (1987): 173–229.

SOHMER, S.H., and R. GUSTAFSON. *Plants and Flowers of Hawai'i.* Singapore: Times Editions, 1987.

STONE, C.P., and J.M. SCOTT, eds. *Hawai'i's Terrestrial Ecosystems Preservation and Management.* Coop. Natl. Park Resources Stud. Unit, Univ. of Hawaii, 1985.

STONE, C.P., and D.B. STONE, eds. *Conservation Biology in Hawai'i.* Honolulu: Univ. of Hawaii Press, 1989.

TERNES, A., and C.M. SIMON, eds. "Hawaii: Showcase of Evolution." *Nat. Hist.* 91.12 (1982): 1–72.

WAGNER, W.L., D.R. HERBST, and S.H. SOHMER. *Manual of the Flowering Plants of Hawai'i.* 2 vols. Honolulu: Univ. of Hawaii Press and Bishop Museum Press, 1990.

REFERENCES ON HAWAIIAN ARTHROPODS

CARSON, H.L. "Tracing Ancestry with Chromosomal Sequences." *Trends Ecol. Evol.* 2 (1987): 203–207.

CHRISTIANSEN, K.A., and P.F. BELLINGER. *Insects of Hawaii. Vol. 15. Collembola.* Honolulu: Univ. of Hawaii Press, 1992.

DEMANCHE, S.E.L., and M.N. HAPAI. *Insects: Hawaii Nature Study Program Teacher's Guide.* Honolulu: Univ. of Hawaii, Curriculum Res. and Development Group, 1980.

HARDY, D.E. *Insects of Hawaii. Vol. 10. Diptera: Nematocera—Brachycera.* Honolulu: Univ. of Hawaii Press, 1960.

HARDY, D.E. *Insects of Hawaii, Vol. 11. Diptera: Brachycera II—Cyclorrhapha I.* Honolulu: Univ. of Hawaii Press, 1964.

HARDY, D E. *Insects of Hawaii. Vol. 12. Diptera: Cyclorrhapha.* Honolulu: Univ. of Hawaii Press, 1965.

HARDY, D.E. *Insects of Hawaii. Vol. 14. Diptera: Cyclorrhapha IV.* Honolulu: Univ. of Hawaii Press, 1981.

HARDY, D.E., and M.D. DELFINADO. *Insects of Hawaii. Vol. 13. Diptera: Cyclorrhapha III.* Honolulu: Univ. of Hawaii Press, 1980.

HOWARTH, F.G. "Hawaiian Terrestrial Arthropods: An Overview." *Bishop Museum Occas. Papers* 30 (1990): 4–26.

HOWARTH, F.G., and G.W. RAMSAY. "The Conservation of Island Insects and their Habitats." *The Conservation of Insects and their Habitats.* Edited by N.M. COLLINS and J.A. THOMAS. London: Academic Press, 1991: 71–107.

KANESHIRO, K.Y., and C.R.B. BOAKE. "Sexual Selection and Speciation: Issues raised by Hawaiian *Drosophila*." *Trends Ecol. Evol.* 2 (1987): 207–212.

MONTGOMERY, S.L. "Carnivorous Caterpillars: The Behaviour, Biogeography and Conservation of Eupithecia (Lepidoptera: Geometridae) in the Hawaiian Islands." *GeoJournal* 7.6 (1983): 549–556.

NISHIDA, G., and S.E. MILLER. "The Hawaiian Terrestrial Invertebrate Database." Honolulu: Bishop Museum, Dept. of Entomol., 1990. Unpublished.

OTTE, D. "Speciation in Hawaiian Crickets." *Speciation and its Consequences.* Edited by D. OTTE and J.A. ENDLER. Sunderland, Mass.: Sinauer Assoc. Inc., 1989: 482–526.

PERKINS, R.C.L. "Introduction to Fauna Hawaiiensis." Vol. 1:xv-ccxxvii, edited by D. SHARP. Cambridge: Cambridge Univ. Press, 1913.

SHARP, D., ed. "Fauna Hawaiiensis." 3 vols. in 18 pts. Cambridge: Cambridge Univ. Press, 1899–1913.

SUMAN, T.W. "Spiders of the Hawaiian Islands: Catalog and Bibliography." *Pacific Insects* 6 (1964): 665–687.

SWEZEY, O.H. *Forest Entomology in Hawai'i.* Bishop Museum Spec. Publ. 44, 1954.

TENORIO, J.M. *Insects of Hawaii. Vol. 11, Supplement. Diptera: Dolichopodidae and Appendix (Phoridae).* Honolulu: Univ. of Hawaii Press, 1969.

THORNTON, I.W.B. "The Psocoptera of the Hawaiian Islands, parts I and II. Introduction and the Non-endemic Fauna." *Pacific Insects* 23 (1981): 1–49.

WILLIAMS, F.X. *The Insects and Other Invertebrates of Hawaiian Sugarcane Fields.* Honolulu: The Hawai'i Sugar Planters' Association Experiment Stn.,1931.

WILLIAMS, F.X. "Biological Studies in Hawaiian Water-Loving Insects," parts IIID, IV, and V. *Proc. Hawaiian Entomol. Soc.* 12, pts. IIID, IV and V (1944): 149–200.

ZIMMERMAN, E.C. *Insects of Hawaii Vol. 1. Introduction; Insects of Hawaii Vol. 2. Apterygota to Thysanoptera; Insects of Hawaii Vol. 3. Heteroptera; Vol. 4. Homoptera: Auchenorhyncha; Vol. 5. Homoptera: Sternorhyncha.* Honolulu: Univ. of Hawaii Press, 1948.

ZIMMERMAN, E.C. *Insects of Hawaii. Vol. 6. Ephemeroptera-Neuroptera-Trichoptera, and Supplement to Volumes 1–5.* Honolulu: Univ. of Hawaii Press, 1957.

ZIMMERMAN, E.C. *Insects of Hawaii. Vol. 7. Macrolepidoptera; Vol. 8. Lepidoptera: Pyraloidea.* Honolulu: Univ. of Hawaii Press, 1958.

ZIMMERMAN, E.C. *Insects of Hawaii. Vol. 9. Microlepidoptera.* Honolulu: Univ. of Hawaii Press, 1978.

INDEX OF SCIENTIFIC NAMES

Ptycta 23

R
Rhynchogonus 23, 50
Rhynchogonus giffardi 32, 114
Rhynchogonus koebelei 114, 115
Rhynchogonus molokaiensis 112
Rhynchogonus simplex 32, 33
Rhynchogonus species A 116
Rhynchogonus species B 116, 117
Rhynchogonus species C 118, 119
Rhynchogonus species D 119
Rhynchogonus stygius 116
Rhynchogonus tubercullatus 114
Rhynchogonus welchi 114
Rhyparochrominae 94
Ruspolia 46

S
Saicella species 90
Saldula 47
Saldula oahuensis 86
Scaptomyza 23
Scaptomyza deludens 150
Schrankia species 138
Scolopendra subspinipes 43
Scotorythra 23
Semiothesa abydata 39, 126
Sierola 23
Spelaeorchestia koloana 43, 68
Speovelia aaa 47, 86
Spheterista species 119
Stenotrupis prolixum 112

T
Telmatogeton torrenticola 142
Tetragnatha 23
Tetragnatha brevignatha 64, 65
Tetragnatha quasimodo 64
Thaumatogryllus cavicola 82
Thaumatogryllus species 13, 27, 46, 82
Theridion grallator 60, 61, 62, 63

Thetella 46
Thyrocopa 23
Thyrocopa apatela 120, 121
Thyrocopa gigas 52
Titanochaeta bryani 150
Trupanea denotata 144
Trupanea species A near *cratericola* 144
Tyrannochthonius 42

U
Udara blackburni 39, 139
Udea 23
Udea eucrena 122
Udea species near *pyranthes* 122, 123
Udea swezeyi 122

V
Vanessa tameamea 39, 52, 58, 60, 140, 141
Vespula pensylvanica 31

X
Xyletobius 23
Xylosandrus compactus 50

ACKNOWLEDGMENTS

We especially acknowledge Dr. Steven L. Montgomery and the late Dr. Wayne C. Gagné for collecting and providing many of the specimens shown in these photographs, and for inspiring our study of Hawaiian arthropods. We also thank G.M. Nishida for information in the tables; G.A. Samuelson for information on the beetles; R.C.A. Rice for specimens and information on beetles and crickets; K. Sattler for information on moths; and J.W. Beardsley, J. Dobbs, N.L. Evenhuis, R. Gillespie, S. Gon III, D.G. and N.C. Howarth, K.Y. Kaneshiro, S.E. Miller, S.L. Montgomery, G.M. Nishida, G.A. Samuelson, F.D. Stone, and J. Strazanac for providing data and many helpful suggestions for the book. We also thank the many people who, over the years, have shared with us their knowledge of Hawaiian natural history.

PHOTO AND ILLUSTRATION CREDITS

Bishop Museum: Page 8 (from Sohmer & Gustafson, 1987).

Betsy H. Gagné: Nos. 121 and 122.

Francis G. Howarth: Pages 6 (top), 11 (bottom), 49, and 56; Nos. 10 and 11.

Mike Kido: Page 16.

Steven L. Montgomery: Pages 24, 25, 36, and 51; Nos. 2, 29, 36, 82, 83, 85, 136, 139, 140, and 156.

Gordon Nishida: Page 11 (top).

David Preston: No. 123.

Edith Sattler: Nos. 110, 111, 114, 115, 117, 118, 120, 124, and 142.

Sohmer & Gustafson, 1987: Pages 8 and 12.

William P. Mull: All other photos except those credited above.